Sometimes it seems like all the logical arguments for traditional marriage were trumped by these two words: marriage equality. Sean McDowell and John Stonestreet provide an important perspective with compelling prose and selected interviews. They explain how we got to where we are today, set forth the case for marriage, and provide an action plan for the twenty-first century. You need this book in order to understand what is going on and in order to be an effective witness for Christ.

Kerby Anderson
President, Probe Ministries
Host, *Point of View* radio talk show

The marriage terrain has undergone a seismic shift over the past decade, leaving Christians disoriented and confused about where to turn for help. Thankfully, John and Sean have written a clear and reliable guide to all of the major questions. This is a book that trades in shrillness for substance, offers wisdom and not platitudes, and counsels faithful hope, rather than despair.

Matthew Lee Anderson
Lead Writer at MereOrthodoxy.com
Author, *The End of Our Exploring: A Book about Questioning and the Confidence of Faith*

This well-written work is a sobering, yet hopeful, examination of the factors that have led to our current social ethic on sex, marriage and identity, as well as an insightful map showing the Christian community our pathway back to regaining our cultural influence. This book is a must read for everyone who is seriously seeking to move from simply winning arguments to the gospel call of winning souls.

Chris Brooks
Campus Dean, Moody Theological Seminary—Michigan
Senior Pastor, Evangel Ministries, Detroit, Michigan

Sean McDowell and John Stonestreet are two of the brightest minds on the planet. But their best quality is love. They love Jesus. And they love people. So with keen intellects and love-filled hearts, *Same-Sex Marriage: A Thoughtful Approach to God's Design For Marriage,* was written. This is an important book! Buy one for yourself and a fri~~end~~

Derwin L. Gray
Lead Pastor, Transform~~ation~~
Author, *Limitless Life: You~~r~~* ~~Futu~~r Future

Spectacular! This is the book on same-sex marriage that we've all been waiting for. A clear, winsome and engaging treatment of one of the most important topics of our time.

Eric Metaxas
Bestselling Author, *Bonhoeffer* and *Amazing Grace*
Cohost, *BreakPoint*

Biblically-informed, pastorally-focused, and culturally-sensitive, Sean McDowell and John Stonestreet have given us a superb guide to the same-sex marriage debate. They not only show us what's right and wrong, but they also offer us a way forward in repentance and faith. Read this as soon as possible.

C. Ben Mitchell, Ph.D.
Graves Professor of Moral Philosophy, Union University, Jackson, Tennessee

John Stonestreet and Sean McDowell aren't content to win an argument about the present controversies. They also seek to cast into the future a compelling case for the necessity of marriage as the one-flesh union of a man and a woman for life. This book is packed with truth, hope, joy and gospel love. Read it and start thinking about how to articulate the good of marriage, no matter how confused the culture may be.

Russell D. Moore, Ph.D.
President, Ethics & Religious Liberty Commission,
Southern Baptist Convention, www.russellmoore.com

So what do you think about same-sex marriage? It's not *if* Christians will have to share their views on same-sex marriage but *when*. Many Christians don't know what to say. Finally there's a book that helps Christians think clearly, compassionately and courageously about how they should engage the new reality of same-sex marriage. This book also offers practical wisdom for navigating difficult personal and family situations. When students raise the question of how to think about same-sex marriage from a Christian perspective, this will be the first book I recommend!

Jonathan Morrow
Speaker and Author of *Questioning the Bible: 11 Major Challenges to the Bible's Authority*
Founder of Think Christianly (http://thinkchristianly.org)

The mainstreaming of homosexuality is such a contentious issue in society today primarily because it creates a very radical view of human sexuality and the family that no society has ever faced before. Those of us trying to navigate this issue in thoughtfulness and truth have a valuable gift in what McDowell and Stonestreet provide for the Church in this important book. They are uniquely well-versed to provide this wisdom and insight, both from much study and experience as thought leaders.

Glenn Stanton
Director of Global Family Formation Studies, Focus on the Family

Always be ready to give a . . .

THOUGHTFULRESPONSE
CULTURERELEVANT**BIBLICAL**TRUTH

SAME-SEX
MARRIAGE

A Thoughtful Approach to
God's Design for Marriage

Sean McDowell
& John Stonestreet

BakerBooks
a division of Baker Publishing Group
www.BakerBooks.com

Published by Baker Books
A division of Baker Publishing Group
P.O. Box 6287, Grand Rapids, MI 49516-6287
www.bakerbooks.com

Printed in the United States of America

Library of Congress Cataloging-in-Publication Data is on file at the
Library of Congress, Washington, DC.

All Scripture quotations, unless otherwise indicated, are taken from the
English Standard Version, Copyright © 2001. The *ESV* and *English Standard Version*
are trademarks of Good News Publishers.

Other versions used are
KJV—King James Version. Authorized King James Version.
THE MESSAGE—Scripture taken from *THE MESSAGE.*
Copyright © by Eugene H. Peterson 1993, 1994, 1995, 1996, 2000, 2001, 2002.
Used by permission of NavPress Publishing Group.

14 15 16 17 18 19 20 | 10 9 8 7 6 5 4 3 2 1

Contents

Part 1:
What Marriage Is and Why It Matters

The issue of same-sex marriage is a major shift for our society and presents a major challenge to Christians who embrace a biblical view of sex and marriage.

Not long ago, same-sex marriage was unthinkable, even to many within the homosexual community. Today, it seems all but inevitable. It is important to understand the shift in context to demonstrate how quickly and comprehensively change has happened.

Most of the noise and heat between advocates and opponents of same-sex marriage boils down to differing answers to one question: What is marriage? Interview: Dr. Glenn Stanton on how same-sex marriage changes what we know about marriage.

To understand what God thinks of same-sex marriage, we must first determine what God thinks of marriage.

If the biblical witness is true, we should expect to find reasons and evidence for God's view of marriage outside of Scripture. Interviews: Jennifer Marshall and Austin Nimocks on same-sex marriage and religious freedom.

Part 2:
What We Can Do for Marriage

How then should Christians live in a culture that embraces same-sex marriage? How do we remain both faithful to truth and loving to people in the days to come?

Dedication

*To our children—Scottie, Shauna and Shane (Sean), Abigail,
Anna and Ali (John)—with prayers that each of you will be courageous,
truthful and loving representatives of Jesus Christ no matter what
is happening in the culture around you*

Introduction

No one wants to be a bigot.

Well, maybe *some* people relish accusations of intolerance and hate, but not most of us. We just want to be liked, and we try to treat people fairly. We want to be good citizens and good neighbors.

For those who follow Christ, the standard is even higher. We are not only supposed to like others; we are supposed to love others as we love ourselves. We shouldn't just tolerate other people; God commands us to care for them and to actively promote their good.

This is not, however, the Christian's current reputation. According to Dave Kinnaman and Gabe Lyons, "When you introduce yourself as a Christian to a friend, neighbor, or business associate who is an outsider, you might as well have it tattooed on your arm: anti-homosexual, gay-hater, homophobic." Kinnaman and Lyons's book *UnChristian: What a New Generation Really Thinks about Christianity . . . and Why It Matters* summarized a survey taken by young Americans. They were asked what came to mind when they thought of the word "Christian." For over 90 percent of those surveyed, "anti-homosexual accurately describes present-day Christians."[1]

As Christians, we might think this is unfair. "Look at our soup kitchens and adoption rates," we say. "How about our track record in disaster relief and sponsoring hungry children?" And we add, "Who is leading the fight against worldwide sex trafficking?" Yet, our appeals seem to fall on deaf ears. The fact remains that we are far better known for being against gays than being for people.

In response, some Christians (as well as media pundits) say it's time to leave this issue alone, lest we continue our journey toward the dustbin of history. They say that to die on this hill, as culture continues its march toward full acceptance of the lesbian, gay, bisexual, transgender, and questioning (LGBTQ) lifestyle, is to become irrelevant or, even worse, relegated to the category of the culturally "unclean" with white supremacists and Klan members. The single worst thing we can do, if the critics are correct, is to oppose same-sex marriage. Denying "marriage equality" will only guarantee that any vestiges of public influence the Church has left will die a humiliating and very public death.

We understand this perspective. Each of us has already faced both personal and public scorn for things we have said and written on the topic of homosexuality and marriage, though these topics have not been a major focus of our teaching and speaking. Our respective ministries are dedicated, in different ways, to promoting the public proclamation of the gospel. The vast majority of our time is spent teaching that Christianity is intellectually defensible and compelling in light of the evidence, arguments and alternatives.

The risk in writing a book like this one is that it may become known exclusively as one that is *against* same-sex marriage. That's not what we are after. Rather we are *for* the hope Christ offers the world. So, why write this book at all? Why risk being marginalized to the wacky right-wing fringe of society? Why go against the overwhelming tide of culture to speak out on this one issue?

The simple answer is, it matters. Voices on both sides of the issue agree that the push to legalize same-sex marriage will go down as one of the most significant social revolutions in human history. That may sound like hyperbole, but the speed at which same-sex marriage went from unthinkable to unquestioned is unparalleled in modern memory. A shift of these proportions leaves an enormous cultural wake. Given what is at stake, we can stay silent no longer.

What exactly is at stake? Proponents of same-sex marriage compare their cause to the great human rights campaigns of history. Their media allies agree, and often anything related to same-sex marriage overshadows other newsworthy items such as economic depression, unemployment, international conflicts, persecution of religious minorities, and erosion of religious liberty. The impact of this social revolution is being felt as widely as corporations, churches, conferences, camps, nonprofit organizations, counseling programs, colleges and universities, photographers, the Department of Defense, adoption agencies, bakeries, reality television shows and state laws.

Frequently, pronouncements are made from town councils, Supreme Court justices, pastors, media moguls, athletes, celebrities, special interest groups and the White House telling folks to comply "or else." In a rush to accommodate, policies and priorities are rearranged in classrooms, courtrooms, sitcoms, denominational leadership, corporate charities, the U.S. military and insurance plans.

On the other hand, opponents of same-sex marriage warn of everything from the end of Western civilization to the loss of the

American way of life; from the hypersexualization of school children to the targeted elimination of any who resist the agenda. Predictions range from the likely to the bizarre. For many on this side of the debate, confidence in public opinion is gone, replaced with a fear of what now seems inevitable.

And yet, even if the dire predictions are true, they will not happen overnight. Life still goes on the day after every ballot initiative and Supreme Court decision. We'll still be here. We'll still wake up, get out of bed, go to school or work, interact with our neighbors (including our LGBT ones), have deeply held differences of conviction with one another, and live in whatever society we have made for ourselves.

The question we try to answer in this book is, "What now?" How can the Church best respond in the midst of this changing environment? What will Christian faithfulness look like once new definitions of marriage and sexuality replace those that have undergirded our society for so long? We can't pretend it's not happening, nor can we just dismiss its significance and hope to move on. We need to think through what these huge changes will mean. We need to know how to carefully think through the issue of same-sex marriage, how to talk about it with others, and how to live in a culture that considers it normal.

It's an enormous cultural challenge but could also be an incredible opportunity for God's people to flourish in their witness to the truth of the gospel. As Christians, we believe there is something more profoundly true than any and all cultural fads. We believe the kingdom of God, as initiated in the life, death and resurrection of Jesus Christ, is the real story of history. Civilizations come and go. Governments rise and fall. Cultures change and change again. But the kingdom of God has no end.

We, therefore, refuse to despair. To say or think, "All is lost," is to say or think something that is not true. As Richard John Neuhaus profoundly put it, "We have not the right to despair, for despair is a sin. And . . . we have not the reason to despair, quite simply because Christ has risen."[2]

That doesn't mean there's no cause for concern. There is, and it's not just what's "out there" in the culture. There's plenty to be concerned about "in here," in the Church. So in the pages ahead, we'll ask whether the American Church is prepared for what is now required of us. We'll need, through the power of the Holy Spirit, clarity of thought and courageous convictions. Unfortunately, our discipleship priorities for the last several generations do not reflect the Church's need to reflect the Kingdom.

Anemic understandings of the Christian life will be exposed for what they are when basic Christian beliefs that were once shared by everyone are instead rejected as dangerous and hateful. Platitudes such as "Love like Jesus!" will need to be bolstered by theological content, and bumper sticker proclamations of "coexistence," will be proven silly and naïve.

This is no time to quit. In this book, we are after clarity of thought and clarity of action: right thinking and right doing. Christians who fail to think well about key cultural issues never rise above infectious confusion or unprofitable anger. A church that hides from cultural conflicts or chooses to do nothing will become culturally captive and will effectively abandon people to be victims of bad ideas. Love of God demands truth, and love of our neighbor demands action.

Part One of this book is devoted to how we should think about the issue of same-sex marriage. In the first chapter, we begin to explain why this issue matters. We'll take a quick tour of how sharply the culture has shifted toward homosexual behavior, sexual identity and same-sex marriage. In the next two chapters, we will look at what the Bible has to say about marriage. Along the way, we will answer the increasingly common challenge that the Bible really doesn't have much to say about same-sex marriage.

We often hear that the only objections to same-sex marriage are rooted in religious bias. This is not true. We are unapologetically Christian, but in the fourth and fifth chapters, we will lay out the prudential case for keeping marriage as the union of one man and one woman.

In chapter six, we will show how same-sex marriage fits into a larger historical context. This shift has not been as quick as many think, but in fact, has been inevitable in light of a new orthodoxy about humanity and human sexuality that has arisen in the last century. Ideas have histories.

Part Two of this book describes what the truth about marriage demands of us. Ours is not the first generation of Christians to face cultural challenges. We are not the first to have our deeply held convictions questioned and attacked. Like those who have gone before us, we must wrestle with our Christian responsibility in light of cultural realities.

So, in chapter seven, we will offer what might be called "a theology of action." We believe the greatest threat to the Church in our day is not same-sex marriage but the feeling of hopelessness that comes from thinking we are "on the wrong side of history." The Christian need not be concerned with "winning." Our hope is in Jesus Christ. Besides, claims that same-sex marriage is "inevitable" exhibit more hubris than certainty.

In chapter eight, we will examine the history of the gay movement, which has been incredibly effective in shifting cultural opinion and initiating change. There's much we can learn, both in terms of what happened and how culture might be shifted again.

Among the lessons to be learned from the gay movement are the power of admitting past mistakes and changing from the inside out. Of course for the Church, we first learn this from Scripture. What's happening inside the Church is far more important than what is happening outside, and when we haven't done what we ought to do, the gospel gives us a clear next step. So, chapter nine is a chapter of self-examination.

Chapter ten will begin the action plan. Here we will look at what Christians can specifically do about the issue of same-sex marriage. The next chapter suggests what Christians can do to begin restoring marriage from the degradation it has suffered. This may seem unrelated, but it's not. Stopping same-sex marriage is only part of the problem. Fixing marriage is the rest.

In chapter twelve, we will get specific. We will discuss, "What do I do if . . ." Across culture, we face specific situations that will challenge our convictions and our relationships. We need to be ready.

After talking through the *what*, it's critical to discuss the *how*. Finally, in the conclusion, we will suggest four postures that are critical to Christian faithfulness. As recent events demonstrate, the coming years will likely not be pleasant for those who are committed to traditional marriage. Yet, Scripture still calls us to gentleness, courage, joy and hope.

Throughout this journey, you'll hear not only from us but also from others. We took our toughest questions to the best voices we could find. Their contributions are both insightful and practical.

Now, let's get started.

Part 1

What Marriage Is
and Why It Matters

This triangle of truisms, of father, mother and child, cannot be destroyed;
it can only destroy those civilizations which disregard it.

G. K. Chesterton[1]

 # What Just Happened to Our Culture?

We're not that old. Really, we aren't. We were both born around the mid-seventies, which basically makes us children of the eighties. Our earliest cultural memories include big hair, *The Cosby Show* and Ronald Reagan. We graduated high school in the early nineties. Those were the days of the Dream Team, grunge rock, a booming economy and political debates over the meaning of "is." (Thanks, President Clinton.)

But homosexuality was not really on our radar. Sure, that sort of thing happened in San Francisco and Greenwich Village but not in rural Virginia or Orange County. And same-sex marriage? Well, that wasn't on *anyone's* radar in the '80s and early '90s. Even most gay activists considered it either out of reach or a bad idea.[1] It was never discussed in our youth groups or at the Christian colleges we attended because, well, it really wasn't being discussed *anywhere*. And remember, we're not that old.

For a culture, however, a lot can change in just a few decades. Twenty years can be the difference between notepads and iPads. Thirty years can be the difference between Elvis and Eminem. Forty years can be the difference between Jim Crow laws in the South and the first black President of the United States.

In fact, in just the last 10 years we've seen big changes in how we think of gender, sexuality and marriage in America. I (John) remember when I realized just how much had changed. In the summer of 2004, I led a youth camp that featured the incredibly moving testimony of a man who had left a radical homosexual lifestyle to follow Christ. He was now married with children. His story, which he dubbed "From Prostitute to Pastor," sparked dozens of questions, which continued over the next several days, even after he had left the camp. So, student after student approached me with their question, opening with, "I've got this friend who is gay."

That's when it hit me. I would have *never* said that when I was growing up because neither I nor anyone I knew of in our small Christian community had friends who were openly gay. We had our suspicions about a few classmates, but they weren't our friends. Mostly, they were, shamefully, the targets of our ridicule.

It wasn't because I was this "holier than thou" prude, either. Plenty of my friends were sexually promiscuous, addicted to drugs, alcoholics, cheaters, bullies or all-around jerks. But gay? No way.

But for the high school and college students we work with today—even the most conservative, churchgoing ones—homosexuality is not a far-off issue like it was for us. This issue is as up-close and personal as their family members, Facebook friends or themselves. And for many, legalizing same-sex marriage competes with the fight against human trafficking as being the social justice issue of their generation.

Plus, they cannot even remember television or film without prominently gay characters on their favorite shows. Other than maybe *Duck Dynasty*, homosexuality is an ever-present and normal part of their collective media intake. Our favorite shows had the occasional homosexual character in the background, and there was the occasional "edgy" film like *Philadelphia* that explored what we thought to be a fringe group of society. But today, same-sex couples are just there, like other couples, on dates, in committed relationships, with children, and maybe even married.

It's Not the '80s Anymore

In 1996, only 27 percent of the United States population supported same-sex marriage. That same year, President Bill Clinton signed the Defense of Marriage Act (DOMA), essentially instructing all aspects of the federal government to only recognize a marriage between a man and woman. In 2013, the U.S. Supreme Court struck down Section 3 of DOMA as being unconstitutional, and public approval for same-sex marriage jumped to 53 percent of the population, including 73 percent of 18- to 29-year-olds. Eighty-three percent of voters today believe that same-sex marriage will be legal across the United States within 5-10 years, though many of those doubt it will take even that long. As David Von Drehle wrote for *Time* magazine in March 2013, "Yesterday's impossible now looks like tomorrow's inevitable."[2]

According to Von Drehle, the swift embrace of same-sex marriage is nothing short of a "seismic shift" in American culture, and one that is "as rapid and unpredictable as any turn in public opinion."[3] He's certainly right. Yet, if there were indicators of this social revolution when we were in high school (there were), we missed them.

We remember laughing with all of our friends at Jerry and George trying to dispel the rumor they were gay while quickly adding, just to be safe, "Not that there's anything wrong with that."[4] Five years after that *Seinfeld* episode (and the same year the foursome finally got what they deserved in the series' last episode), another show debuted as part of NBC's coveted "must-see TV" Thursday night lineup. It was called *Will and Grace*.

According to Vice President Joe Biden, this show is the reason America eventually accepted same-sex marriage. In a 2012 appearance on *Meet the Press*, Biden opined, "I think *Will and Grace* probably did more to educate the American public than almost anything anybody's ever done so far." Most people would not have considered *Will and Grace* an educational program, but Biden was right. And just a few days after Biden's comment, Barak Obama became the first U.S. President to officially endorse same-sex marriage.

While we've not been able to confirm that President Obama was indeed a fan of the show, it's difficult to overstate its power in reshaping the cultural imagination. Plenty of other shows, dating all the way back to Billy Crystal on *Soap*, had gay characters, but *Will and Grace* was about gay life. Here, in this New York City apartment, gay life was not only funny; it was *normal*.

Well, at least Will was normal. Grace? Not so much, but Will was always there to help her navigate her messy heterosexual lifestyle. And a new trend was set.

Just five years after Will began solving Grace's problems, five guys with a "queer eye" began helping "straight guys" fix their various fashion, home and social faux pas. The results, we must admit, were often impressive and made "metrosexual" a household word.

Two years later, the Academy heaped adulation and multiple Oscars on Ang Lee's *Brokeback Mountain* for "courageously" teaching that little things like marriage, children and commitment shouldn't stop true love. Yet, for all the cowboys who were scandalized by that movie, very few teenagers were scandalized by the highly sexualized high school world of *Glee,* just four years later. The *90210* kids we watched in the 1990s may have been more glamorous, but the kids from northwest Ohio's William McKinley High School were far more progressive about who could love whom. Plus, they sang about it, even changing personal pronouns whenever necessary.

That same year, *Modern Family* debuted for the grown-ups. Like *Will and Grace,* many Americans found the show very funny. Unlike *Will and Grace,* they also found it familiar. Maybe the various incarnations of family reminded them of their own lives or maybe their neighbors. Either way, it was obvious that a same-sex couple that was married and raising children just didn't come across as edgy anymore. Somewhere around 2010, at least when it came to homosexuality and same-sex marriage, it seemed television was no longer driving culture but reflecting it.

It's been quite a journey from *The Cosby Show* to *Seinfeld* to *Will and Grace* to *Modern Family.* Older Americans reminisce about *Leave It to Beaver* and *I Love Lucy,* but, clearly, it's not the '50s anymore. It's not even the '80s (or the '90s) anymore. As it is on television, so is life for the larger culture.

The American Psychological Association considered homosexuality a mental disorder until 1973. The World Health Organization only removed the label in 1990. Today, of course, it's a settled matter in academic circles and professional associations that homosexuality is merely one of many legitimate and natural sexual orientations. In fact, we hear it may even have benefits that heterosexuality does not have.[5] All that remains is to work out and promote its social acceptance and to deliver the commensurate rights that are now due, which primarily has been defined as the right to marry.

When Evan Wolfson wrote what was one of the earliest cases for same-sex marriage in a Harvard Law School thesis in 1983, even most gay activists found the idea to be too radical and too unrealistic.[6] Five years later, Andrew Sullivan's article in *The New Republic,* entitled "Here Comes the Groom," attracted more support.[7] Today, of course, it is assumed by most that the issue is settled or at least inevitable. The major debate now is what on earth to do with those who don't acknowledge same-sex marriage as legitimate. Many publications, such as *Slate* magazine, have now moved on to making the case for polygamous and polyamorous marriage.[8] (Seriously, wouldn't it be at least a little ironic if polyamory were recognized as a legitimate marriage expression before spell-check recognized it as a legitimate word?[9])

Of all the cultural mood swings on homosexuality and marriage, it is the legal one that attracts the most attention. As recently as 1986, the Supreme Court ruled that the "right to privacy" applied to intimate, *marital* relations but specifically did not apply to intimate, *homosexual* relationships. Thus, it upheld the rights of states to pass and uphold laws prohibiting homoerotic activity, such as sodomy.

That 1986 decision (*Bowers v. Hardwick*) was overturned by another five to four decision in 2003, in the case of *Lawrence v. Texas*. Justice Kennedy wrote that states could not legislate intimate behavior between consenting adults. In his strongly worded dissent, Justice Anton Scalia wrote that by this decision, the Supreme Court had "largely signed on to the so-called homosexual agenda." A year later, Massachusetts became the first state to legalize same-sex marriage.[10]

When the Supreme Court delivered its decision on DOMA in 2013, they clearly avoided issuing the sort of sweeping national ruling for which gay marriage advocates had hoped. Instead, they pushed the issue back to the states while ruling that the federal government must recognize any marriage, including same-sex ones, sanctioned by a state. In December 2014, New Mexico became the sixteenth state to legalize same-sex marriage, with other states following quickly behind it. In most cases, it's being forced on states by judicial fiat; in a few cases, by popular vote. Either way, it's happening.

So, that settles it, doesn't it? In light of this history, it seems obvious same-sex marriage is coming whether we like it or not. It's on an unstoppable trajectory toward universal acceptance. "Opposing it is pointless," we hear and then echo. "That ship has sailed," said one youth pastor to an apologist friend of ours. "I'm not going to talk about it anymore."

On one hand, it's hard to imagine what that youth pastor could mean by such a silly statement. *Not* talking about it isn't an option for anyone living on planet Earth, much less someone who is employed to work with young adults and their parents. On the other hand, it's easy to see what he means. Like many, this youth pastor finds it pointless to resist same-sex marriage, especially with a younger audience, even if he has private convictions against it. It's best if he just embraces it and moves on, lest it becomes a barrier to ministering to students.

Other Christians go further. For them, it's not about getting out of the way of historical inevitability. It's about justice. Equal rights and human dignity are the worthiest of social causes and have been the reasons cited most loudly and frequently by "marriage equality" advocates. Those who resist same-sex marriage do so out of what Justice Kennedy called "animus" toward homosexuals.[11] They are, we often hear, on the wrong side of history and morality. Even so, some Christians argue we should be on the front lines of this holy cause to remove systemic discrimination and violations of human dignity. After all, that's what Christians have always done. That's what Jesus would do.

Embedded in that reasoning, however, is an "if." And we'd say a rather big "if." G. K. Chesterton once said something to the effect that one should never tear a fence down unless he or she knows why it was put there in the first place.[12] This was especially true, suggested Chesterton, "in the matter of reforming things." After all, it is quite possible to create a host of other problems while trying, even sincerely, to address another.

So, we must ask: Is there an essential nature to marriage that would, by definition, exclude certain consensual adult unions? Or, in other words, are there legitimate reasons that the fence of marriage was placed where it was for virtually every civilization until this one? We think the answer to both of these questions is yes, and that's why we stand on the side of the fence that we do.

We should all remember, no matter which side of this issue we are on, that this debate invokes incredible emotional intensity. Thus, it's been mostly characterized by vitriol. But this issue is far too important for that. The ideas and individuals at stake deserve better than hurled clichés, accusations, raised voices and name-calling. As Ravi Zacharias often says, "When you throw mud, you not only get your hands dirty, but you lose a lot of ground."

To pretend as if everyone on one side of the fence only hates gays, and everyone on the other side only hates God, morality, America or all three, is simply wrong and uncharitable. That isn't to suggest no one carries ill intent. Some on both sides of the issue do. Yet this is not what motivates us. Our parents taught us always to believe the best in others.

For Sean, learning to believe the best in others was especially formative, given that his dad is one of the foremost public defenders of Christian truth in recent memory. But Josh McDowell both taught and modeled that even if we disagree with someone, we should still give that person the benefit of the doubt. This is what we aim to do in our lives and in this book. We don't question the motivation of those with whom we disagree. We won't call them names, and we won't question their character. In fact, we believe that most are driven by what they think is compassionate and true. But this doesn't mean we won't take a firm position on what we think is right.

In this book, of course, we clearly take a stand on the issue of homoerotic behavior and same-sex marriage. We do so because we *must*, according to our conscience before God. To paraphrase Luther, "Here we stand. We can do no other." As Christians, we may not always like where our faith demands that we stand, and yet, we must. Even so, civility need not be sacrificed on the altar of truth nor truth sacrificed on the altar of civility. Truth given in love is what our Savior demonstrated, and what He demanded from His Church.

Accordingly, we'll need to talk not only about what Christians are called to think on this issue but also how we are expected to live out our convictions. We will do so in the pages ahead. But first, we will carefully look at where this marriage fence has been historically placed and why it has been placed there. In the next few chapters, we humbly suggest that the ability to articulate the basic truths about marriage, given our current cultural situation, is every Christian's responsibility.

2

Beyond the Noise, ⟪ ⟪ ⟪
Beyond the Heat:
Starting at the Right Place

The idea of same-sex marriage elicits more fear than thoughtfulness. We've seen bakers in Colorado, photographers in Arizona and rednecks in Louisiana face the consequences of expressing their convictions publically, by word or deed. To even admit doubts on the issue is to put oneself at risk. For many elites, the cultural debate is over. All that's left to decide is what to do with those who refuse to participate.

Others are just angry. Most of us don't like to be told what we can and cannot believe or say, as is so often the case these days. At the same time, many in the homosexual community feel hurt and angry over injustices they've endured, which can be both perceived and real. Their newfound cultural power carries with it a great temptation for retaliation.

As Christians, we need to be clear about our beliefs regarding marriage and any responsibilities these beliefs imply. In the middle of all of this hurt, anger, vitriol and fear, it is difficult to have a rational, thoughtful conversation about all that's at stake. Where do we begin?

The Central Question

Our good friend Scott Klusendorf, perhaps the most articulate spokesperson for the pro-life position in America, is often asked to debate pro-abortion advocates at universities and other public settings. He will often begin his argument this way: "We should allow abortions in all nine months of pregnancy as is currently legally allowed in the United States." At this point, all the pro-lifers who thought Scott was on their side are confused until he says the magic word "if." "Abortion should only be legal *if* it can be demonstrated that the unborn are not members of the human family."

Scott uses this rhetorical strategy because he understands how often emotional platitudes, clichés and sound bites drown out the foundational issues that are at stake in our most important cultural debates. In the case of abortion, talking about women's reproductive "rights" or pregnancies of unusual circumstance, although important, is often used as a red herring to prevent the main issue from ever being discussed: What is the unborn? Clarifying whether the unborn are human beings of equal worth and due dignity, in turn, clarifies the entire debate.

There's also a big *if* when it comes to same-sex marriage. And like abortion, the *if* in this debate is one of definition. Same-sex marriage should be legal *if* marriage is only a way that the government acknowledges feelings of love and affection between people. *If* that's all there is to marriage, keeping marriage from same-sex couples would be discrimination along the lines of racism and sexism or perhaps based on religious convictions that are not shared by everyone.

But what if, on the other hand, marriage is about more than just our feelings of love and affection, as important as they are? For example, what if it matters in marriage *who* is in love and not just *that* they are in love? That seems true enough at first glance, doesn't it? After all, there are many other couples, like those who are underage or closely related, who are not allowed to marry.

And, what if it has more to do with *just* being in love? Being in love certainly matters, and love and affection are among the greatest experiences humans have. But no one ever asked us about the sincerity of our love when we applied for our respective marriage licenses. Not one government official in the county clerk's office said to us, "Now wait a minute. Are you *sure* you are in love? Here, take this test in the latest *Cosmopolitan* magazine to prove you *really* love each other." Perhaps that sort of thing happens in some states but not in California or Tennessee. We were asked whether we were related to our fiancée and whether we were of the age of legal consent, but never how strongly we felt about our spouses.

So, obviously, there is much that is already assumed about marriage in our society that is often overlooked in the current debates. The ways in which societies regulate marriage reveal a good bit about what we think (or at least used to think) marriage is. Along these lines, we'll argue, like many others have before us, that marriage has a number of obvious and essential purposes that distinguish it as a relationship unique from all others. That's why, before we decide who's in and who's out and before we start leveling accusations of discrimination, we need to understand that the central question is, what is marriage?

The Thing About Discrimination

Societies always privilege some relationships to qualify as marriage, while they discriminate against others. The distinctions made between relationships can either be based on *essential* qualities or *arbitrary* qualities. Distinctions based on essential qualities are not made in order to insult or trivialize the quality or sincerity of a couple's love and devotion for one another. Rather, distinctions based on essential qualities are those that are made between certain relationships that qualify as marriage and others that don't. They are based on the sort of unique relationship marriage is and the purposes it alone serves.

Of course, many societies, throughout history, have discriminated against relationships that in every essential way qualified as marriage. Examples of this kind of discrimination, such as Jim Crow bans on interracial marriage, are typically aimed at the people in a society who are considered to be less valuable than others. This sort of discrimination is *arbitrary*.

Our point is that, as strange as it sounds to say it, not all discrimination is wrong. It's often appropriate and necessary. Neither of us would be allowed to join a MOPS[1] support group or to order McDonald's coffee at the senior citizen price. But that doesn't bother us. That kind of discrimination isn't arbitrary. It's based on a set of essential qualifications that mothers and senior citizens have that we don't. If, however, a stressed-out dads group refused to admit Sean because of his faux hawk hairstyle or a McDonald's refused to serve coffee to John because he's balding, that would be arbitrary discrimination. And, it would be wrong.

But homosexual orientation isn't like a hairstyle, you say. It can't be changed. That is, of course, a hotly debated point. And as important as the truth about orientation is, it is irrelevant to the point we just made. When it comes to marriage, the difference between essential discrimination and arbitrary discrimination has to do with *what marriage is*, not what sexual orientation is. There are plenty of loving and committed relationships that are acknowledged as being loving, committed, natural and healthy by everyone but still wouldn't be called marriage. Even if there is nothing morally wrong with homoerotic behavior, determining whether a relationship should be considered a marriage requires that we first answer the question, what is marriage?

In this book, we argue that marriage is an institution created by God for unique and particular purposes. These purposes are evident even if God's existence is denied. Therefore, it only makes sense that the vast majority of societies throughout history (and their governments) would privilege and protect certain relationships as marriage and not others because of the particular goods that only these relationships provide to these societies.

It may be that your reaction to that last paragraph is, "Huh?" Don't worry; we'll unpack it in the next several chapters. But before we do, here's one quick point of clarification: Just because we argue that marriage should be restricted to heterosexual relationships does *not* mean we think same-sex romantic relationships should be criminalized. It doesn't even mean that we think loving, committed homosexual relationships should have no legal protections when it comes to property, inheritance, and care of partners. Many want to cloud this debate with false choices, but we reject those. One can think that marriage should be only between a man and a woman without thinking homosexuals should be the target of prosecution or discrimination. We, in fact, abhor mistreatment of gays as we do the mistreatment of *any* human beings. Yet this issue is about one simple question that often gets lost in all of the noise: What is marriage?

Where We Look for Answers

In the coming chapters, we will look at the definition of marriage from two angles. First, we will look to the Bible. Where should followers of Jesus stand on same-sex marriage and why? What does the Bible have to say about all of this?

"Ha!" you may be thinking. "There go those Christians, trying to impose their morality on everyone else. Not everyone believes the Bible, so why would we base our laws on *it*? You wouldn't like it if we based our laws on the Qur'an, would you? And besides, what about the separation of Church and state?"

These are good questions. That's why we also look at marriage from extra-biblical sources. As we'll see, there are substantial non-religious reasons to define marriage only as the union of one man and one woman.[2]

But we decided to start with the biblical witness about marriage for four reasons. First, we are Christians, and Christians are the primary audience for whom we've written this book. Every major orthodox stream of Christianity claims that what the Bible says about any given issue is very important. We would say it's *most* important.

Second, even nonbelievers should be aware of what the Bible teaches. Jesus is rightfully recognized as one of the greatest (if not *the* greatest) ethical teachers of all time. His witness is found in the Bible. And given its influence on our literature, history and culture, it's vital to know what the Bible says.

Third, many Christians say that marriage is, to quote a phrase we hear often, not a "hill worth dying on." Some argue this on theological grounds, claiming that cultural concerns are secondary to the gospel proclamation, while others are merely being pragmatic. They say that it's too controversial and will distract people from hearing the message.

Either way, we disagree. The theological objection is grounded in bad theology. It assumes that the message of Scripture is only one of personal salvation. It is not. The message of Scripture is the proclamation of the Kingdom of God. The great Dutch theologian and statesman Abraham Kuyper wrote, "No single piece of our mental world is to be hermetically sealed off from the rest and there is not a square inch in the whole domain of our human existence over which Christ, who is Sovereign over all, does not cry, 'Mine!'"[3]

The pragmatic concern is irrelevant if the Bible portrays marriage as being even moderately important. Theologian Owen Strachan wrote that we should be "spider-sense wary about the 'Christian teaching is a stumbling block to the gospel' argument." He said that it is "a devil's bargain."

There is nothing in Scripture to apologize for; there is nothing to feel bad about. God doesn't need new PR. He doesn't need people to be embarrassed for him. He's not looking for super-authentic apologizers who can clear up the scandal of his claims of cosmic dominion. He hasn't overestimated; his calculations of rightness have not been proven wrong. He isn't red-faced in heaven in the face of modernity, or postmodernity, or whatever else will come down the pike. He's not scared by current events. His angels are not hastily recalibrating the kingdom program to retrofit it for an age that has caught them sleeping in the control room . . . Heaven does not quake at earth. It's the other way around.[4]

"Render to Caesar the things that are Caesar's," Jesus says, "and to God the things that are God's."[5] Before we conclude that some cause isn't worth it, we have to discern if God agrees. If the biblical testimony requires us to conclude that marriage belongs to the state to define it in whatever way it pleases, then so be it. But if the biblical testimony identifies marriage as belonging primarily to God and not *established* by the state but *recognized* by it, that's another matter altogether.

Fourth, too many Christians are left speechless when they hear someone claim that Abraham's and Solomon's polygamy is proof there is no "biblical ideal" of marriage, that the Bible rarely talks about homosexuality and never condemns loving homosexual relationships, or that David and Jonathan were more than "just friends." Biblical illiteracy is both prevalent and infectious today and often leaves Christians embarrassingly unprepared for the far-too-common-but-misguided game of swapping proof texts. Simply put, Christians should know what the Bible says about something as important to the human experience as marriage and sexuality.

But What Does the Bible Say?
Some are likely to object that we can't actually know what the Bible says. After all, well-meaning Christians throughout history disagree on what the Bible says about all kinds of things. And the few passages that deal with homosexuality were written for another time and place, not for today. After all, there are also restrictions on shellfish and certain fabrics in the Bible. Just as we ignore those passages because of historical context, we should do the same with those dealing with homosexuality.

It's interesting that despite the vast disagreement throughout the history of the Church on a whole list of items, there has been virtually no disagreement on the definition of marriage or the sinfulness of extramarital sexual activity. Only in recent decades has there been any sort of attempt to argue that the Bible does not expressly condemn sexual relationships of every kind outside the context of marriage.[6] If anything should be considered culturally dependent, it's not the biblical teaching on sexuality but the current questioning of it.

Still, it can be difficult to tell the difference between what the Bible teaches and what it doesn't teach. So before we jump in, here's a little clarification about how we are approaching the Bible in this book and why.

T. S. Eliot once observed that whenever we see something new, two questions need to be asked. One is, "What can it do?" or perhaps, "What can be done with it?" The other question is, "What is it for?" This question, Eliot suggested, should be answered first.

The reason this question comes first is because purpose determines function. The why needs to be determined before we start deciding the what. Before we decide what we should *do* with something, we need to know what that something is *for*.

A few years ago I (Sean) called my Internet service provider for help with my home computer. Right before hanging up, I asked the operator, "What are the craziest questions you have ever received from people on how to work a computer?" His response was hilarious. "One lady asked me how she was supposed to use the foot pedal on her computer." Can you guess what the foot pedal actually was? The mouse!

"Another young man complained that the cup holder was too small," he continued. (Yep, he was trying to use his DVD-ROM drive.) "And another lady walked around her house closing all the open windows because the computer screen said, 'Close all open windows.'"

These honest and hilarious mistakes were due to a failure to properly understand what different parts of a computer are *for*. The mouse is not meant to function as a foot pedal, and the DVD-ROM is not supposed to hold cups. The computer is designed to function in a certain manner, and when it is not used in that manner, confusion often results.

This also applies to marriage. We are not intending to trivialize the importance of marriage by comparing it to a computer. We simply want to emphasize that the only way to know what we should and shouldn't do with marriage, like whether to expand it to include same-sex couples or restrict it to exclude interracial couples, is to first answer the question, "What is marriage *for*?"

Beginning with the purpose of marriage not only lifts the debate above personal emotions and political correctness, but it also brings necessary context to a common argument that many Christians find difficult to answer. The Bible barely mentions homosexuality, this argument goes, and there was no understanding back then of committed, loving, homosexual relationships or of sexual orientation. Therefore we are to conclude that the whole issue of homosexuality is not the big deal that we think it is today.

The obvious assumption here is that the number of biblical mentions is an indication of its biblical importance. But that's just not true. For example, the Bible only mentions a few times that human beings are made in God's image and that we should care for the environment. Does this mean the Bible fails to take a moral stance on the dignity of humans or the treatment of the planet? Of course not.

While the Scripture does include specific pronouncements about particular acts, it also lays out a comprehensive story of the world. Many have rightly summarized this story as creation, fall and redemption.[7] In light of the way God originally made the world, we can better see human relationships in the larger context of what God intended them to be. From this angle, we can see when and where things go wrong and what it means for them to be made right again.

Too often, Christians on both sides of the debate bring up competing proof texts without considering the way God made the world in the first place. Having a larger context in place helps us clarify specific biblical passages (like Leviticus 18 or Romans 1). It's a better way to read the Bible, a better way to ensure we are thinking biblically, and a better way to answer the question, what is marriage?

So in the next chapter, we look to the Bible. But we won't start in Leviticus or Romans. Instead, we go back to the very beginning.

How Same-Sex Marriage Changes What We Know About Marriage

INTERVIEW WITH DR. GLENN STANTON

If marriage really is the force for good that many say, then wouldn't it accomplish the same good for the LGBT community? Why not allow it then?

It is not just coincidence or tradition that marriage has at all times and in all societies been a relationship between men and women. Marriage exists because of the dual, gender-distinct nature of humanity. And because of these very important and consequential differences, marriage is needed in all societies to accomplish four primary goals:

1. To regulate sexuality—both in terms of procreation, but also to protect it from opportunism and the abuse of people, primarily women.
2. To socialize and domesticate the male nature—marriage settles a husband down and focuses him on caring for his wife, the mother of his children, and their common children.
3. To protect women from opportunistic men and empower them relationally—relationships where commitment is expected favors women. Relationships where commitment is not expected favors men.
4. To ensure that a child gets from both parents the attention, care and provision he or she requires until young adulthood is reached.

It is a large and open question as to whether men can socialize other men and women can protect other women. The fact is—born out in ample and diverse research, and reported in the summer of 2013 in the *Atlantic*[8]—that women in "long-term" committed relationships break up at dramatically high rates, even in countries that are remarkably gay-affirming. In fact, research conducted in Scandinavia shows that same-sex male relationships break up at twice the rate of hetero-cohabiting and married relationships. And lesbian relationships break up at more than twice the rate of gay relationships. They are not stable—primarily because women tend to be more relationally intense, and men tend to temper this in women. Women tend to amplify it, and few relationships can survive such emotional and relational intensity. Research on lesbian relationships confirms this.

Likewise, long-term gay male relationships are extremely likely to allow for outside sexual relationships—based on certain rules the couple intentionally establishes. This indicates that men do not typically motivate their male partners to settle down sexually like heterosexual women are able to do. And, clearly, this is very different from the understanding of sexual fidelity universally implied to marriage.[9]

Why is one-man/one-woman marriage unique from other loving, committed relationships? Do both genders really matter that much to marriage?

There are so many reasons why this matters. Husbands and wives influence each other differently and in very important ways in which other relationships do not; and they influence their children in different and essential ways that are necessary for healthy child development, as I explain in my book *Secure Daughters, Confident Sons*. Man and woman coming together in the marital union, the most intimate, secure, long-lasting and consequential way that two can come together, really creates a full, human whole—it brings together into a cooperative relationship the two distinct and necessary parts of humanity. This is no small thing.

During many years of work on this topic, and many media interviews with leading journalists, I was often asked whether male and female are *really* necessary for the family. I respond to this question by asking them to consider their own place of work: "What if your newspaper/television station/etc. was comprised of only male or female employees. Do you think that would have any influence, for good or bad, over the kind of product your team produces?" They usually don't answer or will quietly assert, "I see your point." Then I ask, "If male and female are essential to bring different perspectives, skills, insights and wisdom to your work, how much more is that needed for the family?"

Simply put, male and female, and the influence they have on one another, are important to the family in light of the unique and necessary gifts, experiences and perspectives they bring to the table.

Many same-sex marriage advocates point to the high divorce rate. If heterosexual marriage has been such a disaster, why not allow gays to see if they can do better with marriage?

I get this question a lot, and the proper response is to address the nature of the question itself because it is a slippery one. This is not avoidance, but uses basic logic.

It goes like this: When asking for something that you don't think you'll get, appeal to the poor way those you are asking have handled what you want. This puts them into a corner, giving the questioner a seemingly moral upper hand. But turning the tables like this avoids addressing the nature of the question itself. It's similar to the kid who gets busted by his parents for smoking pot. He responds, "How can you tell me no, when you did that very thing when you were my age?" And, surprisingly, parents feel shut down by this. But isn't the question about whether or not same-sex marriage is a good idea?

Imagine that all heterosexual marriages always worked and remained intact for life. Would that be an argument *against* same-sex marriage? Would same-sex marriage advocates have less of a position to argue from if this were the case? Of course not, because it is irrelevant to the issue they are proposing. So, the question that points out the high divorce rate for heterosexual marriage really is not an honest question—even if the person asking it is sincere. And, of course, the research I mentioned earlier shows that legally recognized gay and lesbian relationships are actually dramatically less stable and lasting than either cohabiting (which are famously unstable) or married heterosexual relationships.

Glenn T. Stanton is the director of Global Family Formation Studies at Focus on the Family and the author of six books on various aspects of the family. His two most recent are *Secure Daughters, Confident Sons: How Parents Guide Their Children into Authentic Masculinity and Femininity* (Multnomah, 2011) and *The Ring Makes All the Difference: The Hidden Consequences of Cohabitation and the Strong Benefits of Marriage* (Moody, 2011).

What Is Marriage?
Part One:
What God Thinks

Many people note that Jesus said nothing about gay marriage. This is true. He did, however, speak about marriage. In response to a less-than-sincere question that came from some of the Pharisees regarding divorce, in Matthew 19, Jesus revealed there was something more fundamental than the letter of the Mosaic law. Most important when considering marriage and divorce, Jesus said, is what is true about marriage "from the very beginning."[1]

By taking His questioners back to the Garden, Jesus grounded His ideas about marriage in what we might call "God's created *intent.*" That shouldn't surprise us since Jesus was not only present at the creation of the world but also was responsible for it.[1] It is notable, however, that He answered the question in the way that He did. The Pharisees wanted to know how Jesus understood what was written about marriage *in Jewish law.* In response, Jesus placed both the law and its instructions on marriage within the larger context of what God had intended in creation.

We'll come back to His specific teaching about marriage in this passage, but let's state the obvious. Jesus cared about marriage as well as the form marriage takes. If Jesus found God's intent for marriage important, then we should too.

In fact, considering God's created intent is the only way to confirm what is true about marriage. To borrow a phrase, the world in which we live is "not the way it's supposed to be."[2] The creation is tainted by sin and so are our minds and hearts. Just as a junkyard is not the best place to learn how to build cars, so too our cultural and personal preferences aren't the best place to learn how to build marriages. Sure, we'll find some original parts, but we'll also find rust, dirt, dents and disrepair. Historically, Christians have understood that even our most sincere inclinations, affections, urges, institutions and ideas—though natural and normal to us—have been infected, broken and twisted by the fall.

So, from Genesis 3 on, we should remember that the Bible does not *endorse* everything it *reports*. Many passages are descriptive but not prescriptive. God's command that Hosea marry a prostitute, for example, is not a universal command.

Some argue that because the Bible is not prescriptive on everything, it is not prescriptive on anything, including homosexuality.[3] But this is not the case. Each of the three main "chapters" of the larger biblical story—creation, fall and redemption—implies that God embedded created norms into the world He made. These norms are, as Jesus demonstrated in His answer, *prescriptive*. The fall corrupts these norms but doesn't dismiss them. Christ's redemptive work restores them but doesn't remove them. As Matthew Lee Anderson says, "Creation is the context wherein the meaning of redemption is grasped; redemption clarifies, restores and deepens the goodness of the original creation."[4] Anderson concludes that, unless we keep in mind the creation norm, "any account of human sexuality will necessarily be stunted."[5]

So with that in mind, let's examine how the Bible describes both the design and the purpose of marriage. To do this, we will take a walk in the Garden.

Filling and Forming

The Bible opens with these familiar verses: "In the beginning, God created the heavens and the earth. The earth was without form and void, and darkness was over the face of the deep" (Genesis 1:1-2). The rest of the chapter describes what God does to fix the formlessness and emptiness. Simply put, He forms and fills.

"Let there be light," God says (1:3), and the empty darkness is filled. "And God separated the light from the darkness" (1:4). In other words, God gives the light shape. He fills, and He forms. He fills the world with new things: stars, land, the atmosphere, animals. Then He shapes these things: He separates day from night,

He tells the water how far it can go, He divides the waters in the expanse above from the waters below and He places the plants, trees, fish and beasts into distinct "kinds." God's world is shaping up rather nicely.

God accomplished His filling and forming work by speaking. He says it and, *poof*, it happens. Everything obeys Him and becomes what He tells it to become. Even "nothing" obeys Him when He tells it to become "something." God is so thoroughly and completely in charge, nothing exists without His command. God's language is described by a repeated rhythm that holds the first chapter of Genesis together: God says, "Let there be," and it was so. God looks over what He has made and pronounces it "good."

"Let there be. . . and it was so. . . it was good . . ." over and over and over. Just as this rhythm is getting stuck in our heads, it changes. As Genesis 1:26 reports, human beings are not created by fiat command. As everything else has been. Instead of a "Let there be," God utters a "Let us make." This is new. The next chapter provides details: "then the LORD God formed the man of the dust from the ground" (2:27). God not only employed a different language, He employed a different process as well.

What God created next is unmatched by anything He has created thus far. "Let us make man in our image, after our likeness," He said. "And let them have dominion over the fish of the sea and over the birds of the heavens and over the livestock and over all the earth and over every creeping thing that creeps on the earth" (1:26).

Don't miss this very important point: The absolute Ruler of everything decided to make other rulers. The great Sovereign, who up to this point in the story has showed Himself completely in charge and without rival, created human beings to bear His image and to "rule" for Him in the world. They are not puppets nor have they been granted tourist visas for paradise. They have work to do.[6]

Incredibly, their work is the sort of work that God has been doing. Note the instructions: "Be fruitful and multiply and fill the earth and subdue it" (1:28). Just as God did, they are to fill the earth. Just as God did, they are to bring order to disorder. Just as God did, they are to bring life and fullness. In other words, they too, like the One whose image they bear, are to fill and form. They are to begin this work in the Garden and continue it throughout the earth.[7]

"But, what's all this have to do with marriage?" you ask. Good question. You may have noticed that the earth is a big place. Not only is the earth too big for Adam to form without help, but also he certainly cannot fill it alone either! Not to worry because God has a solution that is revealed as the story's focus shifts to the first couple.

Alone, Not Lonely

Just after a poetic summary of the story thus far, Genesis 2 further clarifies about the first man and the significant work he is to do. The verdict is that he is "alone," and this is "not good." He needs help, and because no bird or beast is up to the task, God makes him a suitable helper. You know the story: deep sleep, rib taken, woman made. The man is so impressed with God's work that his response sounds like he is breaking into song. They become "one flesh," which, Genesis 2:24 states, is the model for all subsequent "one flesh" unions.

What does it all mean?

Note that nowhere in this story are we told that the man is *lonely* and in need of *companionship*. Rather, God's verdict is that he is *alone* and in need of a *helper*. God has instructed him to "fill and form" the entire planet. He can't do this alone. So, God gives him help.

It's curious that Genesis specifically says that the animals were not suitable helpers (2:20b). That sounds silly to us today, but think about it. Why aren't animals the sort of help man needs? From the earliest civilizations, animals have been known to be quite useful. They've been used to build up, to tear down, to carry, to till, to farm and to perform all kinds of culture-building activities. They aren't bad as far as the "forming" work goes. But what the animals couldn't help with is the "filling." The woman, of course, could (and did). Together, the two would procreate, an act which produced other fillers and formers who would also procreate and so on and so on. The brilliant design of man and woman could accomplish God's created intent for His image bearers.

Within this larger context, we can begin to answer that most important question: What is marriage? We can't do this by proclaiming fundamentally different relationships to be marriage. We can only do this by determining *the purpose of marriage*. Biblically, God established marriage as the institution through which He would equip humanity to populate and cultivate His creation. (And because He's kind, He made it pleasurable and fulfilling.)

What about companionship, you ask? Companionship is certainly *a* purpose of marriage. It's just not the *only* purpose of marriage. If marriage were *only* about companionship, there would be nothing to distinguish it from other very important, human unions.

In marriage, companionship is a motivator to bring couples together, but it's not *the only reason* they are together. God did not create the woman merely to keep the man company. After all, in the Garden, the man shared company with God. God created the woman to be "a suitable helper."

Other human relationships offer companionship in different forms, but only marriage can make a man and woman "one flesh" in every sense of the word: emotionally and physically; in body and in purpose. Husbands and wives are more than companions. They are *helpers*. Together, they produce, protect and preserve future generations of image bearers who will continue the human task of "filling and forming" God's world.

"But marriage isn't necessary for someone to be a parent," you say. That is obviously true, but it is the *best* relationship for protecting and preserving future generations. Think about it: If most people lived in committed, heterosexual, marriage relationships, would that make the future of our civilization more or less secure both in quantity and quality? What if, on the other hand, most people avoided marriage? Marriage, when properly practiced, brings *security* and *stability* to a society that no other relationship can bring.[8]

We realize that for those who have experienced divorce or abuse, often do not see marriage as a good option. Because failed marriages are the source of so much *insecurity* and *instability*, it is tempting to blame marriage itself. But the fact that a failed marriage leaves such a negative wake for those involved helps explain why healthy marriages leave such a positive wake. Marriage is a unique relationship.

In the next chapter, we'll look at evidence for that claim, but for now, it's important to realize the biblical blueprint for marriage: Two become one not *just* for happiness or emotional fulfillment, but also for a good that is greater than themselves. No couple's marriage is, biblically speaking, just about them. It's about future generations. It's through marriage that God arranged to perpetuate civilization. That's what marriage is *for*.

In light of all God did to bring the first man and woman together, Genesis 2 closes with a definitive statement that this created norm is forever embedded by God into the human story (2:24). And it's on this conclusion that Jesus grounds His reply to the Pharisees when they question Him about divorce. "Have you not read," Jesus asks, "that he who created them from the beginning made them male and female, and said, 'Therefore a man shall leave his father and his mother and hold fast to his wife, and the two shall become one flesh'? So," Jesus concludes, "they are no longer two but one flesh. What therefore God has joined together, let not man separate" (Matthew 19:4-6).

What Makes a Marriage?

In this God-given, Jesus-endorsed design, we find three essential characteristics of marriage.

First, *marriage is two human beings becoming one in every way possible*. No living thing, until God made woman, was capable of becoming one flesh with the man. God pronounced the absence of woman as being "not good" because it left man alone and incapable of accomplishing God's purposes for humanity in His world (2:18). In marriage, two become one, united in every possible way: mind and body and purpose.

Second, *marriage is oriented toward procreation*. The act of two becoming one flesh makes God's intent, that humans should "fill" and "form" His world, possible. God wanted more humans. Rather than create them, He chose to equip His image bearers with the biological potential to procreate them. Of course, not every married couple is able to procreate. We'll look at that objection more closely later in this book, but our point here is that Scripture sees marriage as being closely tied to procreation.

Procreation explains why sexual intercourse is seen throughout Scripture, as well as in most societies, as the act that consummates marriage. This also explains why sexual activity outside of marriage is seen throughout Scripture as sinful.[9] Because sexual intercourse is the only biological process that leads to procreation, this implies that marriage requires gender diversity.[10] Same-sex relationships, even if they are sincere in love and affection, cannot meet this basic requirement, though opposite-sex relationships, including interracial ones, can.

Third, *marriage comes with an expectation of permanence*. While the language of "leaving" and "holding fast" and "one flesh" in the Genesis account implies marriage is a permanent relationship, Jesus' words are explicit: "What therefore God has joined together, let not man separate" (Matthew 19:6). When His questioners respond with the policies of divorce from Mosaic law, Jesus responds that divorce was an *accommodation* provided because of the hardness of their hearts. But Jesus quickly adds, "from the beginning, *it was not so*" (Matthew 19:8, emphasis added). He understood marriage as a permanent arrangement.

The Rest of the Story

We've argued that the biblical view of marriage is clear, both from Genesis and from Jesus' endorsement. It is God's means of enabling human beings to fulfill their purpose of "filling and forming" God's world. Even if cultural and personal baggage makes marriage difficult, it doesn't make it something else.

There are three things to add:

First, from a biblical perspective, marriage is an institution created for all humans and not only for Christians. Christians and non-Christians can fulfill the design we've described above. The Church didn't create marriage, but rather, it recognizes it as a gift of God for His image bearers.

Therefore, we shouldn't think of marriage as a political institution that belongs to the state. It is a pre-political institution. The state doesn't create marriage; it can only recognize it. The state, despite all its efforts, will never be able to redefine marriage. Marriage will always be what marriage was created to be, no matter what activist judges, runaway legislatures or majority of voters decide. As our friend Dr. Frank Beckwith says, "You can eat an ashtray, but that doesn't make it food."[11]

Second, the fact that the first couple sinned does not negate marriage's design. The consequence of the first sin is not that God removes the dignity of the human task to fill and to form His world. Instead, the job must now be done through pain and toil (see Genesis 3:16-17). The purpose remains the same.

On a purely experiential level, we can see how this is true. We've watched our wives give birth multiple times and are very content that God gifted them with that side of procreation! Yet, neither of our wives would say, "I wish I hadn't gone through that." They look back on giving birth as one of the most meaningful and deeply fulfilling experiences of their lives. So do we (though we remember far less discomfort than they do).

In a similar way, people often derive deep and meaningful satisfaction from very difficult work: climbing a mountain, building a skyscraper or university, writing a novel, or seeing a child graduate from college. Arthur C. Brooks has argued that once basic needs are met, a primary key to happiness is the ability to earn success.[12] There is still a deep, innate desire in people to fulfill their God-given purpose.

Since the fall, however, marriage has played an additional role of restraining evil in society. Marriage reminds men and women of their responsibilities as spouses and parents, while tying them to their children. This encourages long-term thinking, curbing the temptation to live for immediate gratification.

Third, marriage not only has *creative* purposes, but it also has *redemptive* purposes. Marriage offers the world a picture of the fidelity, commitment and love that Christ has for His Church. Quoting Genesis and Jesus, the apostle Paul repeats God's created intent for marriage in his letter to the church at Ephesus: "Therefore a man shall leave his father and mother and hold fast to his wife, and the two shall become one flesh" (Ephesians 5:31). He then adds, "This mystery is profound, and I am saying that it refers to Christ and the Church" (v. 32).

Marriage does not lose its importance in the New Testament, rather it is clarified. As created, marriage enabled male and female to reflect God's image together. As redeemed, marriage reflects Christ's love for the Church. As created, marriage enabled God's image bearers to spread His rule over all the earth. As redeemed, marriage disciples both current and future generations to spread the gospel over all the earth. As created, marriage is the foundation of social order. As redeemed, marriage commits us to live and restrain our passions for the good of others.

In no way does this mean that only married people can achieve their human purpose and contribute significantly to God's world. The contributions of widows/widowers, children, teens and other singles are just as important as the contributions of married couples, whether those contributions are made in the Church or in society. However, marriage plays a central role in teaching future generations.

After all, not everyone has had children, but everyone has had parents. Strong marriages strengthen the character of future generations, and everyone, whether married or single, benefits. There is significant extra-biblical evidence that this is so, and it's to that evidence we now turn.

What Is Marriage?
Part Two:
Leaving God Out of It

In his 2013 Supreme Court opinion on the Defense of Marriage Act,[1] Justice Anthony Kennedy implied to the world that anyone who opposes marriage for gays and lesbians does so out of hate and animus. What he failed to mention is that every definition of marriage excludes someone. For example, many advocates of same-sex marriage think marriage should exclude polygamous and polyamorous couples. Just about everyone (thankfully) thinks marriage should exclude underage and incestuous couples. If any and every type of relationship should be called marriage, it's no longer a helpful term. Marriage can't mean everything, or else marriage means nothing.

This is why, as we've said already, the fundamental question in the debate over same-sex marriage is, what is marriage? Unless that is settled, we won't be able to determine which relationships should count as marriage and which shouldn't, or whether a relationship is or isn't being wrongfully discriminated against. Equality under the law is as important a social cause as there is. It is, in fact, a Christian value.

Even the notorious atheist philosopher Friedrich Nietzsche recognized human equality as "another Christian concept" that "furnishes the prototype of all theories of equal rights."[2] More recently, Luc Ferry, also an atheist philosopher, stated bluntly that the Christian notion of equality was "unprecedented at the time, and one to which our world owes its entire democratic inheritance."[3]

To deny equality to others where it is due would be a distinctly anti-Christian thing to do. But the only way to properly apply principles of equality to marriage is to first know what marriage is. After that, we can figure out which laws, ceremonies and public policies best support the institution.

In the last chapter, we looked at how the Bible presents marriage. Marriage was designed by God to thoroughly join two image bearers in a permanent commitment, enabling them to fulfill their purpose of filling and forming God's world. This view of marriage was embedded in creation, according to Jesus, "from the beginning," and is limited in its design to one-man/one-woman unions. Because it is a created norm, it trumps all cultural or personal attempts to alter it.[4] It is the fundamental framework from which the Bible develops sexual ethics[5] and has been the central assumption of historic Christian church teaching on marriage and sexuality.

"But that's just religion," you say. "That doesn't fly in the public square with those who don't accept the Bible's authority." True enough. Historic Christian teaching on marriage and sexuality doesn't seem to hold much authority anymore nor has it influenced public opinion for quite some time. Still, as Flannery O'Connor put it, "The truth does not change according to our ability to stomach it emotionally."[6] The Bible presents its view of marriage as true not only for Jews and Christians but also for all humanity. We should not be surprised, then, to find that what the Bible says about marriage corresponds to what we find in the world around us. And it does. Here's how.[7]

Three Undeniable Facts of Reality

According to Maggie Gallagher, there are three obviously true facts about the world that make the institution of marriage necessary: "Sex makes babies. Society needs babies. Babies deserve mothers and fathers."[8] "Wait a minute," you say. "That's it? That's all she's got?" It sounds far too simple to be all that important, doesn't it?

Simple? Yes. Important? Yes again.

These three facts are *obviously* and *universally* true of every time period and every human culture. Not only are they obviously and universally true, but also they are *simultaneously* true. In other words, every society in human history has to deal with these truths, and they have to deal with all of them *at the same time*.

Think about it. Sexual intercourse between a man and a woman brings babies. Not every time of course but often, and sometimes in spite of efforts to prevent conception. Though artificial reproductive technologies have become more common, sex is still the most common way we get babies. No matter how advanced these technologies become, this is not likely to change. And due to its enduring popularity, it is doubtful people will stop having sex anytime soon.

Of course, not every couple that is having sex will have a baby, but many will. And though not every couple wants a baby, many do. Whatever couples decide to do, the society they live in *needs* babies in order to survive. After all, the mortality rate is 100 percent for everyone. We need replacements.

It follows, then, that societies have a vested interest in the process that most often produces children. That's why every society cares about sex. Societies also have a vested interest in supporting an environment that best *rears* children. That's why every society cares about marriage.

Numerous studies demonstrate that children fare better when cared for by their biological mothers and fathers. A 2008 report published by the Witherspoon Institute entitled *Marriage and the Public Good: Ten Principles* summarizes this data.[9] Children who live with married moms and dads show, on average, advantage in literacy and graduation rates, emotional health, family and sexual development, and behavior as both adults and as children.

So, there you have it. Sex makes babies; society needs babies; and babies deserve mothers and fathers. Historically, marriage is the institution by which societies have recognized and managed these three truths, both culturally and legally. Thus, marriage is a reality that transcends times and cultures. It commits mothers and fathers to each other and to any children who result from their sexual activity. This, in turn, perpetuates society. That's why, as Maggie Gallagher observes, "marriage is a virtually universal social institution."

While marriage is certainly not identical in every society, in every society it serves the role of "bringing together a man and woman into a public—not merely private—sexual union in which the rights and responsibilities of the husband and wife toward each other and any children their sexual union produces are publicly—not privately—defined and enforced."[10] Whew . . . that was a mouthful. Let us explain.

What Happens in the Bedroom Doesn't Stay in the Bedroom

As I (John) work on this chapter, loud music is flooding my hotel room and disrupting my thoughts. I am trying to concentrate, but it's not my fault. Someone is playing the classics: "Brown Eyed Girl," "YMCA," "We Are Family," and of course, "Don't Stop Believin'." It's the obligatory playlist of every wedding reception.

Earlier today in another part of the hotel, a man and a woman stood together in front of family and friends and committed their lives to one another. The bride, I noticed, wore a white dress, as many brides do, even though what it symbolizes is now considered quaint and prudish. She walked down the aisle, the groom met her there and they were married.

I don't know this couple, nor do I know any of the people who are now loudly celebrating their nuptials outside my door. But I do know what's likely to happen between the newlyweds later tonight. Everyone at the wedding, except the children, also knows, as do the hotel employees who are staffing the reception. And we all know that we all know. Even the bride and groom know that we know and yet, for some reason, they still choose to participate publically in a ceremony that announces it to all of us. In any other context, a public announcement that a couple was about to have sex would be, well, creepy. Celebrating would be creepier still. But on a wedding day, there is, rightfully, no shame.

Obviously, a wedding day is not just about sex, even for eager grooms. It's about marriage. And what we described above says a lot about the sort of thing marriage is.

First, marriage unites two individuals in a very powerful and public way. People, from old friends to new acquaintances, will think of the couple together. In many social and legal settings, from now on they will be treated as a single unit. Now there are domestic, financial, conjugal and familial implications. They have some new benefits and responsibilities because of their decision to marry. Together, they are their own entity.

Of course, there are other types of couples who share life together but are not considered a single entity, at least not in the same way. Perhaps two recent college grads, for example, have decided to prolong their roommate arrangement in order to extend the party or cheapen the rent. They share an Xbox and an apartment, but they are not married just because they share domestic life.

Or imagine two elderly ladies who have lived together for nearly 20 years: a widow whose husband succumbed to cancer and her sister. They care deeply for one another, share everything from their most precious memories to a checking account. They have given each other medical power of attorney and haven't missed an episode of *Jeopardy* since 1995. Theirs is a beautifully committed relationship, but it is not a marriage.

Or what of a romantically involved couple who live together? If you didn't know better, you might even guess they were married, but in fact, they just never got around to tying the knot. They love each other, have children, share a mortgage payment and dream of retiring together somewhere on a beach. Despite the strong resemblance of their relationship to marriage, neither the culture nor the law considers their relationship to be marriage because there was no public commitment to be faithful to each other for life.[11]

Marriage is a relationship distinct from all others. Neither proximity nor depth of affection nor a sincere commitment to love each other and stay together for life is, on its own, enough to make a relationship marriage. That marriage is unique has been recognized across times and cultures, not least of which by governments who deem it necessary to regulate and, at times, incentivize it. Yet those same governments don't deem it necessary to do the same with other very real, very substantial relationships.[12]

Somehow, across time and place, the "oneness" of the marital union is recognizable. The couple is "one" in a comprehensive way: in mind, body and purpose. And the couple is "one" in an exclusive way: neither person will be "one" in this way with anyone else as long as their marriage lasts.

Second, marriage marks two people as sexual partners and makes them publically responsible for their sexual behavior. This is important because sex, though (hopefully) done in private, has very public consequences. Forced sex brings fear to an entire community. Procreative sex creates a new life that must be cared for and integrated into the community. Promiscuous sex risks the mental and physical health of many in the community. Underage sex jeopardizes the potential of the community. Marital sex secures the future of the community.

Once someone is recognized as being married, the community, in a limited but very real and non-creepy sense, is made privy to their sexual behavior. The ceremony and the ring are a virtual "do not touch" sign to potential mates. The community knows this person is now accountable to his or her spouse for his or her sexual behavior. Their exclusivity includes their sexual behavior.[13]

Marriage also makes both spouses accountable for any children produced by their sexual relationship. When a baby is born, a mother is always nearby. But there is not always a father nearby. By recognizing and promoting marriage, the community makes it more likely that when a baby is born a mother *and a father* will be nearby. This is good news for the baby, the mother and the community.

In 1992, Dan Quayle was widely denounced for lecturing a TV single mom. Murphy Brown, said Quayle, was guilty of "mocking the importance of fathers by bearing a child alone and calling it just another lifestyle choice." Candice Bergen's character, the object of his scorn, replied mid-show that "it's time for the vice-president to expand his definition and recognize that, whether by choice or circumstance, families come in all shapes and sizes." This very odd conversation between a real-life political candidate and an imaginary television character was one of the definitive moments in the next election.[14]

Writing 20 years later in *The Washington Post*, Isabel Sawhill of the Brookings Institute, noting the explosion of single parent homes and their impact on poverty, concluded, "in the end, Dan Quayle was right."[15] Sawhill caught very little flack compared to Quayle, perhaps because President Obama, just a year earlier, told *Parade Magazine*, "We can do everything possible to provide good jobs and good schools and safe streets for our kids, but it will never be enough to fully make up the difference. That is why we need fathers to step up, to realize that their job does not end at conception; that what makes you a man is not the ability to have a child but the courage to raise one."[16]

But President Obama was only partially correct. Children need more than fathers who are committed to them; they need fathers who are committed *to their mothers*. John Wooden, arguably the greatest coach of any sport of all time, said, "I agree with Abraham Lincoln. He once said that the best thing a man can do for his children is to love their mother."[17] Married fatherhood is one of the many unique and irreplaceable benefits the institution of marriage brings to children and to the wider community.[18]

Third, marriage assumes permanence. The exclusivity of a married couple's "oneness," both sexual and otherwise, is expected to endure. This does not mean, of course, that marriages always live up to the vows taken. It means they should, and that it's a tragedy when they don't.

The expectation that marriage is permanent has a catechizing effect on the community. When successful, marriage commits adults to their families and to their families' futures. Married adults become practiced at thinking about others. This curbs the urge for immediate gratification relationally, sexually and financially. Children raised in this environment learn to not take commitment lightly.

But even a failed marriage, *in a community that thinks it shouldn't have failed*, reinforces the permanence of marriage. For people to learn from their own mistakes and the mistakes of others, they have to recognize that the mistake was a mistake. When failing marriages are considered normal, the cultural trajectory takes a tragic shift. Instead of the next generation thinking, "I don't want that to happen to me," they conclude, "that's just the way marriage is."

This is why the vision of marriage is so important for a culture and is mostly upstream from laws and public policies. A strong marriage culture brings stability to the lives of the individuals who are involved and to the entire community. A weak marriage culture leaves a community without one of its greatest sources of strength and stability. The inherent qualities unique to marriage are not found in other relational and contractual arrangements.

These reasons explain why governments must be, to some degree, involved in marriage. Marriage laws cannot create marriages; they can only recognize them. The best marriage laws protect it for what it is and for the good it brings to the community. "The law," says Maggie Gallagher, "helps to make the 'one-flesh' union real, requiring the state and other institutions to treat the couple as if their marriage really exists."[19]

"But wait," you say. "Is your head in the sand? Marriage looks nothing like the ideal you described." That, of course, is a sad but true observation. So, let's consider it now.

Marriage and Religious Freedom

AN INTERVIEW WITH JENNIFER MARSHALL

Is same-sex marriage inevitable?

No. Most states still have strong marriage laws, and public opinion remains divided. What's more, in too many cases, it's not that the case for marriage has been heard and rejected—it simply has not been heard. All of us have the opportunity and responsibility to explain what marriage is, why marriage law matters for the good of children and society as a whole, and the consequences of redefining it.

After the *Roe v. Wade* decision in 1973, many people thought the abortion question was settled. To the contrary, the pro-life movement has grown stronger each decade, and young people today are more pro-life than their parents' generation. That's the result of sound argument and winsome engagement on the subject. The marriage question demands no less of us today.

How are we seeing same-sex marriage threaten religious freedom at the federal, state and community levels?

The combination of two types of laws is leading to conflicts with religious liberty: (1) redefinition of marriage laws and (2) sexual orientation/gender identity (SOGI) laws. One of the first spheres of conflict is in wedding-related businesses. Government officials have taken action, for example, against a photographer in New Mexico, a florist in Washington State, and a baker in Colorado for declining to use their creative talents to celebrate same-sex commitment ceremonies. Christian adoption agencies have had to shut their doors rather than compromise their religious beliefs in places like Massachusetts, Illinois and Washington, D.C. when government tried to coerce them to place children with same-sex couples. The question now is not just whether or not law will reflect biblical truth about marriage; it's about whether we will have the freedom to speak and to act in accordance with that truth.

Where marriage has been redefined, what can be done to protect religious freedom?

Federal, state and local policy should protect individuals and groups who believe that marriage is the union of a man and a woman. Government should not take adverse action against those who continue to stand for marriage as it has existed for millennia. Policy should ensure that government officials cannot, for example, revoke the tax-exempt status, deny a grant or contract, or otherwise coerce beliefs about marriage. Explicit protections in law should guard religious adoption and foster care agencies' important role serving children in need. At a time when so many children need a loving home, why would policy drive these effective providers out?

What can everyday Christians do to protect religious liberty for themselves and everyone else?

We must speak up now—with reason, good will and confidence. We need to make the case for marriage. One tool to help your discussions with family, friends and co-workers is a short pamphlet titled *What You Need to Know About Marriage*, available at www.heritage. org/marriage. The Heritage Foundation stands for marriage as the union of one man and one woman on the basis of good reason. And it's with good reason that, in jurisdictions that have redefined marriage, we should call for religious liberty protections. The law should reflect the truth about marriage, and we should be free to live consistent with that truth as well.

Jennifer Marshall is the director of Domestic Policy Studies at The Heritage Foundation where she oversees research in areas that determine the character of our culture: education, marriage, family, religion and civil society.

AN INTERVIEW WITH AUSTIN NIMOCKS

What legal steps should churches, non-profits, and business owners take now to protect their religious freedom in light of the growing legalization of same-sex marriage?

Among the many threats to the freedom of today's religious adherents are laws regarding same-sex marriage and protecting the notions of sexual orientation and/or gender identity. Historically, civil laws did not generally impede the ability of churches and religiously motivated non-profit organizations to operate in accordance with their faith beliefs. But as government continues to encroach upon the sovereignty of the societal spheres belonging to the church, family and marriage, organizations and businesses must be more intentional about demonstrating their commitment to biblical values and finding ways to operate within the shrinking legal windows provided for their existence.

Unfortunately, there is no legal silver bullet that guarantees full operational freedom for biblically motivated organizations, whether they have non-profit or for-profit status. (In America, non-profit and for-profit labels impact an organization's tax status, but not its constitutional rights. Our constitutional guarantees do not depend upon an organization's tax status.) However, organizations can take prudent and intentional steps to safeguard as much operational room as possible.

First and foremost, comprehensive updates to constitutions, by-laws, employment practices and other operational policies (where an organization exists on paper) should occur and be written as clearly as possible. Every aspect of the company's policies should be grounded in the biblical principles that animate that policy. Organizations like Alliance Defending Freedom have developed excellent model policies and guidelines for churches and businesses, for-profit and non-profit, to assist them with these tasks. If an organization has a clear and unequivocal written record of who it is, why it does what it does and why it operates in a certain way, it should have a stronger legal footing in asserting claims or defenses grounded in free exercise of religion principles should trouble arise.

What other preparations must Christians make to prepare for threats to their religious freedoms?

Beyond girding up written documents and policies, pastors and business leaders operating with biblical convictions should mentally, emotionally and spiritually prepare to be challenged. Beyond the many existing and growing number of laws that threaten our religious freedoms, there is an increasingly anti-Christian or anti-religion culture animating those laws. At the hands of many same-sex marriage activists, Christians around the world have been challenged as to whether they will publicly proclaim the name of

Christ, and willingly to accept the consequences that may follow. Some have; some have not.

In the United States, Christian counselors, florists, photographers, bakers, bed and breakfast proprietors, wedding venue owners and many others have been directly threatened, attacked or challenged by the new regime of laws promoting various forms of sexual anarchy enacted at the federal, state and local levels. In addition to promoting anti-biblical principles about the nature of who we are as a gendered species and sexual behavior, these laws almost never provide appropriate or comprehensive legal safe harbors for religious adherents. And as legal saturation of these laws continues, we will all soon be challenged by them in one way or another.

Are you prepared to be challenged? Are you prepared to proclaim the name of Christ no matter what troubles or threats befall you? Have you seriously thought about what you would say or how exactly you would handle a circumstance that conflicts with your biblical principles? Are you prepared to actually rejoice if such a trial comes, knowing that the testing of your faith produces perseverance? (See James 1:2-3.) And are you prepared to suffer, and even be jailed, for your biblical beliefs? If you are not, you run the risk of rendering unto Caesar that which is God's. To prepare yourself, you should consider seriously the growing storms that our culture is brewing. Additionally, you should pray regularly for those who are being persecuted—pray for God's strength for their battles, and take on their burdens as your own. If we are truly one body in Christ, then the sufferings of our brothers and sisters are also ours.

What can Christians do to avoid problems down the road?

Most important, we can defy society's expectation of our ignorance. Bullies rarely seek out or pick equal fights. They look for prey—people who don't know their rights or how to articulate them. Do you know what federal law says about the rights of both employers and employees in the workplace? Do you know what categories of discrimination are addressed by both your state and local laws? Do you know how your locality handles zoning and what limitations exist in law to protect religiously motivated employers? Do you know the identity of the state legislators who represent you at home or at work? What about your local politicians? If you answered no to any of these questions, be encouraged. The answers are available and the more you know, the better prepared you will be.

Austin R. Nimocks is senior counsel for Alliance Defending Freedom, one of the foremost organizations dedicated to protecting religious freedom around the world.

What Is Marriage?
Part Three:
The Tale of Two
Definitions

The current battle over same-sex marriage, with all of its accompanying heat, noise and carnage, is a collision of two visions for what marriage is. But this collision predates today's issue of same-sex marriage. According to the authors of *What Is Marriage?* same-sex marriage is "a pivotal stage in a decades-long struggle between two views of the meaning of marriage."[1] At stake are hearts, minds, relationships, families, laws, institutions and entire cultures.

If that sounds overly dramatic, then so did Caitlin Flanagan's 2009 cover story for *Time* magazine entitled "Is There Hope for the American Marriage?" "There is no other single force causing as much measurable hardship and human misery in this country as the collapse of marriage," she wrote. "It hurts children, it reduces mothers' financial security, and it has landed with particular devastation on those who can bear it least: the nation's underclass."[2]

Flanagan caught a good deal of flack for robustly defending an institution many cultural elites think belongs in the dustbin of history. But her conclusion was straightforward:

> The fundamental question we must ask ourselves at the
> beginning of the century is this: What is the purpose of
> marriage? Is it—given the game-changing realities of birth
> control, female equality and the fact that motherhood

outside of marriage is no longer stigmatized—simply an institution that has the capacity to increase the pleasure of the
adults who enter into it? If so, we might as well hold the wake
now . . . Or is marriage an institution that still hews to its
old intention and function—to raise the next generation, to
protect and teach it, to instill in it the habits of conduct and
character that will ensure the generation's own safe passage
into adulthood? Think of it this way: the current generation
of children, the one watching commitments between adults
snap like dry twigs and observing parents who simply can't
be bothered to marry each other and who hence drift in and
out of their children's lives—that's the generation who will
be taking care of us when we are old.[3]

The definition counts, Flanagan says. And as important as court
cases continue to be, this is not merely a legal question. It's a question
that shapes entire cultures, including ours.

Let's take a closer look at these competing definitions of marriage. The one Flanagan describes as "ensuring procreation" is the
one we described in the last chapter. According to Anderson, Girgis
and George, this "vision of marriage [is] distinguished by its compre-
hensiveness." They call it the "conjugal" view of marriage.[4]

The "Old" View of Marriage

In this view, marriage is more than just a metaphorical or rhetorical union. It's an *actual* comprehensive union in every way possible,
not the least of which is sex. Think about it: Both the man and the
woman are distinct bodies, each capable of carrying out every biological function necessary for survival (breathing, digestion, and so on),
completely independent of each other. There is one exception: procreation. During sexual intercourse, the male and female together
perform a biological function neither can perform alone. It's the only
biological function that requires another person.[5]

Marriage commits the couple not only to a single sex act but also
to ongoing sexual acts. They will continue to sexually express the
cooperation and oneness they agreed to when they married. They are,
in an actual sense, one in every way that is possible for them to be one.

Any child produced by their activity fulfills their physical union
(whether or not that child fulfills their wishes). But, even if pregnancy is never achieved, their union is achieved when the biological

function is performed. "It is the *coordination toward a single end* that makes the union; achieving the end would deepen the union but is not necessary for it."[6]

Marriage connects their bodily union with a union of life and purpose. In other words, sex makes babies, but *marriages make families*. Or to paraphrase President Obama, it's not just about having babies; it's about raising them. Marriage orients and commits a married couple to each other and to any child they will produce. "In short, marriage is ordered to family life because the act by which spouses make love also makes new life; one and the same act both seals a marriage and brings forth children."[7]

In this vision of marriage, the connection between marriage and procreation is more than just incidental. The connection between marriage and procreation has been historically assumed in both legal and popular thinking about marriage in the United States.[8] In fact, the track record of the courts was "uninterrupted" in affirming the inherent connection between marriage and procreation until recently.[9]

If this inherent connection exists, excluding same-sex couples from marriage isn't necessarily an act of animus or hate, any more than it would be to exclude college roommates or elderly, single sisters from marriage. They are excluded because their relationship, though sincerely loving and affectionate, just *isn't* marriage. Marriage has a fixed nature, and by definition "is something only a man and a woman can form."[10]

Including same-sex unions may seem like a simple legal matter, but doing so would enshrine in law a different vision of marriage. Same-sex relationships, whether you believe those relationships to be moral or immoral, do not lead to procreation. If marriage does indeed have a connection to procreation, including same-sex unions as being a type of marriage would change the definition of marriage for everyone.

This example offered by Maggie Gallagher is helpful:

There is no reason in the world why we—or the law—cannot redefine "cat" to mean "furry, domestic animal with four legs and a tail." Defining "cat" in this way has certain advantages. It reveals the deep underlying similarities for example between those two formerly opposite classifications: "dog" and "cat." Not to mention "gerbil," "rabbit," and "guinea pig."

What is lost in redefining "cat" in this way?

Well, there is one little thing: we now no longer have a word that means "cat." If we want to speak to each other about cats, we will either have to invent a new term, and hope it will still communicate the full valence of the old word (rich with historic associations and symbolic over- tones), or we will have to do without a word for "cat" at all. One might reasonably foresee, without charting all the particular specific mechanisms, that it might become harder to communicate an idea for which we no longer have any word.[11]

In other words, if every "furry domestic animal with four legs and a tail" is now to be called a cat, what should we call the thing that we used to call a cat? And how could we possibly tell our neighbors that what was once known as their dog was sprayed by what was once called a skunk? Those of us from the '80s and '90s remember similar trouble trying to figure out what to call the artist formerly known as Prince.

In the same way, extending marriage to same-sex couples leaves us without a word for that unique relationship that has always been called marriage. Words are one way we make sense of reality, and a lack of clarity prevents us from understanding. Think about the abortion debate. Are opponents of abortion considered "pro-life" or "anti-choice" (or anti-woman, or anti-reproductive health or religious fundamentalists)? Are proponents of abortion "pro-choice" or "pro-abortion" (or anti-life, or pro-murder, or godless secularists)? Is abortion a health-care issue, the elimination of tissue, or the taking of an innocent life? Words matter.

Regardless of our words, reality hasn't changed: Sex still makes babies, society still needs babies and babies still deserve a mom and a dad. We need a word for the unique relationship that best manages those things in a society. Expanding marriage to same-sex couples leaves us without one.

But that's not all. Especially in the case of marriage, one redefinition leads to other redefinitions. Gallagher explains:

Social institutions like marriage are created, sustained and transmitted by words, and the images, symbols and feelings that surround words. Change the meaning of the word, and you change the thing itself. One thing same-sex marriage indubitably does is displace certain formerly core public understandings about marriage: such as, that it has something to do with bringing together male and female, men with women, husbands and wives, mothers with fathers. Husband will no longer point to or imply wife. Mother no longer implies father.[12]

Redefining marriage redefines parenthood. The domestic arrangements described in a 2009 *Fox News* report is a case in point:

> Cat Cora, star of Food Network's "Iron Chef America," announced Tuesday that she was 4-1/2 months pregnant with a boy. But this is where it gets interesting. Cora's partner Jennifer, with whom she already has two sons, is also pregnant, and due in April, three months before Cora.
>
> "Jennifer and I are thrilled to go through the wonderful experience of pregnancy together. We started the in-vitro process five years ago," said Cora, who is due in July. "This has been a miracle for us and we'll now have 4 beautiful children."
>
> But we're not done. It gets even more interesting. Cora is carrying Jennifer's biological child. And their second child, now 23 months old, was conceived using Cora's egg, but carried by Jennifer. In Jennifer's current pregnancy, both women's embryos were implanted, so they don't know who the biological mother is, and they say they don't plan on doing DNA testing to find out. The same anonymous sperm donor was used for all four pregnancies, making all four kids biologically related. And you thought your family life was complicated.[13]

What is marriage, then, if not the institution it's always been? What defines it, if not essential characteristics like permanence, exclusivity and procreation? The thing that remains is what the authors of *What Is Marriage?* call the "revisionist view."

The "New" View of Marriage

In the revisionist view, marriage is malleable. Marriage is whatever societies make (or remake) it to be. No longer fixed, it adjusts to ever-evolving moral and sexual norms.

In the revisionist view, relational *oneness* is replaced by relational *intensity*.[14] Neither the *kind* of sexual activity nor the *result* of sexual activity is significant in this view. It's only significant that there is sexual activity. Deeply held feelings and sincere intentions legitimize a couple's claim to marriage. Formally, this view divorces marriage from both procreation and parenting.

Proponents of same-sex marriage, like E. J. Graff, readily admit how different this view of marriage is: "Allowing two people of the same-sex to marry shifts the institution's message . . . If same-sex marriage becomes legal, that venerable institution will ever stand for sexual choice, for cutting the link between sex and diapers."[15] Andrew Sullivan agrees and argues that "marriage itself has changed . . . From being a means to bringing up children, it has become primarily a way in which two adults affirm their emotional commitment to one another."[16]

Why discard the historic understanding of marriage for this new one? First, marriage was evolving decades before the noise of recent years. Divorce rates and out-of-wedlock births have been high for a long time, and our culture no longer understands sex and procreation as belonging to marriage. Same-sex marriage advocates found the cultural ground had already been tilled by the birth control pill, no-fault divorce laws and a culture-wide spike in cohabitation. In the wake of these significant developments, the jump to same-sex marriage isn't really much of a jump at all.

But the move away from one definition of marriage does not ensure the success of another. Same-sex marriage is not the default setting that automatically wins if traditional marriage loses. It is an innovation, and therefore, it must be defended on its own ideals and merits.

More important, the failure of traditional marriage in Western culture is not because the conjugal view is flawed, but because we failed to live up to it. It just doesn't follow that an ideal, particularly one with such a stellar track record, should be indicted as a failure because it hasn't actually been applied. A wiser course would be to rebuild the view of marriage that works, rather than to dismiss it.

Second, traditional marriage should be discarded, we are told, because it is, at its root, based in hate or animus toward gays and lesbians. Any truly hateful behavior is inexcusable. However, to use hate as an excuse to dismiss the increasingly sophisticated arguments for traditional marriage is intellectually dishonest and cowardly,[17] and it is a textbook example of the logical fallacy known as *ad hominem* (attacking the character or motivations of those presenting the arguments instead of dealing with their arguments). The motivations behind an argument are irrelevant to its quality. People on both sides of the issue can be motivated by love or hate, but what matters most is whether their arguments are true or false.

There are gays and lesbians who also offer arguments against same-sex marriage.[18] Should their words be dismissed as hateful? The idea that marriage is identified by procreation, exclusivity and permanence isn't partisan musing. It is, we would argue, reality. If not, it must be demonstrated and alternative explanations should be presented.

Another version of this objection is that traditional marriage only exists because of an old-fashioned cultural morality that sees homoerotic behavior as inherently disordered and sinful. History, however, does not support this view. In *What Is Marriage? Man and Woman: A Defense*, the authors state:

> The philosophical and legal principle that only coitus could consummate marriage arose centuries before the concept of gay identity, when the only other acts being considered were ones between a married man and woman. And even in cultures very favorable to homoerotic relationships (as in ancient Greece), something akin to the conjugal view has prevailed— and nothing like same-sex marriage was even imagined.[19]

Third, it's argued that refusing marriage to same-sex couples is discrimination. Rhetorically, this has been the most effective argument in favor of same-sex marriage in popular culture and the courts. Often, restrictions on same-sex unions are compared to bans on interracial marriages.

This analogy falls apart when we remember that interracial marriages *were* conjugal marriages. A male of one ethnicity and a female of another ethnicity can become one in every sense that a couple of the same ethnicity can. And an interracial sexual union is ordered toward procreation and can abide by the same standards of exclusivity and permanence. Bans on interracial marriages wrongfully discriminated against actual marriages.

But same-sex couples cannot procreate nor can they become "one" in the same sense opposite-sex couples can. Thus, maintaining marriage as the union of one man and one woman is wrongful discrimination only if it can be demonstrated that the revisionist definition of marriage is the right one. If the conjugal view is correct, same-sex couples *can't actually be married*. Claiming discrimination assumes a new definition of marriage as proof for the new definition. It's circular reasoning.

At a practical level, redefining marriage based on the sincerity of a couple's commitment or the depth of their affection disconnects marriage from procreation. And if not tied to procreation, why limit it to a couple? What if three people share a sincere commitment and deep affections? In the same name of fairness, marriage would *have to be* extended to consenting polygamous and polyamorous couples. Nor could marriage be restricted from incestuous couples or deeply committed friends. In this view, it's hard to see why *any* committed group of persons should be left out of marriage.

A fourth reason given for same-sex marriage is that adoption and reproductive technologies have already disconnected marriage from natural procreation. That may be true, but societies have never thought that everyone who raises a child has a claim to marriage. For example, two sisters who adopt an orphan, though performing a heroic good for that child, are not thought to be married. Rather, societies recognize that those relationships that *produce* children have a claim to marriage. By doing so, societies endorse the ideal for procreating and raising children while providing for children outside of that ideal.[20]

The conjugal view argues that marriage is tied to the *act* that leads to procreation because it establishes a family for any children who result from that act. Same-sex couples cannot perform this act, and no children result from their sexual activities. If a child is to be produced, a union of a different kind (involving the genetic contribution from other people) is required.

Society's vested interest in heterosexual marriages is tied to the fact that children deserve a mom and a dad. Marriage gives a mom and a dad to children and removes the burden of caring for that child from the society. When families fail, other institutions must fill the gap to care for those children.

In response, same-sex marriage advocates often claim that children fare just as well or even better in same-sex households. But recent research casts doubt on this claim, which is often called the "no difference" thesis. For example, a review of 59 studies, often used to advance the "no differences" thesis, concluded that "not one of the 59 studies referenced . . . compares a large, random, representative sample of lesbian or gay parents and their children with a large, random, representative sample of married parents and their children. The available data, which are drawn primarily from small convenience samples, are insufficient to support a strong generalizable claim either way."[21]

The New Family Structures Study of the University of Texas,[22] which looked at a larger and more comprehensive population sample, suggested significant differences between children of parents who were involved in same-sex relationships and children raised by their married, biological mother and father. In particular, the study showed differences in economic outcomes, involvement in crimes, sexual victimization, sexually transmitted infections, drug use and depression. Admittedly, this study was also limited, but without further data, it is not accurate to claim the "no difference" thesis is a settled science.[23]

A fifth reason given for same-sex marriage has to do with the rare exceptions to the rule. In other words, if marriage is, in fact, inherently connected with sex and procreation, what happens to those couples that cannot actually have sex because of a disability? Are they married? In this case, we would say, as in the case of the elderly who wish to be married beyond the age of procreation, these relationships do not *rearrange* marriage as do same-sex unions. The state's interest, as Greg Koukl explains in a later section of this book, is in preserving the *institutional* identity of marriage. "Pointing at exceptional cases," he says, "doesn't nullify the general rule."[24]

Finally, we often hear that same-sex marriage is not that big a deal. After all, there's no strong moral case for playing *Angry Birds* or watching *Keeping Up with the Kardashians*, but to each his own, right? If there's no harm, why not allow same-sex couples to marry?

The sound bite version of this argument is, "How will my gay marriage hurt yours?" But no one has ever said that the negative consequences would be immediate. Nor, of course, can anyone definitively claim there will be no harm. It simply hasn't been tried before.

That doesn't mean we are going about this blindly. A closer look reveals that same-sex marriage isn't *causing* a radical shift in our understanding of marriage and family; rather, it's largely the *result* of one. The revisionist view of marriage is riding an ideological wave that has reshaped Western ideas about gender, sexuality and human freedom. Same-sex marriage is one of many cultural innovations left in its wake. But this is not a story about the captivity of the Western mind. It's a story about the captivity of the Western imagination. We look at this history in the next chapter.

 The "Cosmological" Shift: How Same-Sex Marriage Got Here

On April 29, 2013, an article on the *Sports Illustrated* website went viral. Jason Collins, an oft-traded and well-traveled center in the National Basketball Association, became the first male athlete active in a major professional U.S. team sport to announce he was gay. LGBT activists, sports legends, celebrities and former presidents lauded the announcement as historic and courageous. First Lady Michelle Obama assured Collins "we've got your back" via Twitter, and her husband personally called and congratulated him.[1]

Most of the media discussion that followed centered on how this would impact the sports world, especially in those sports typically known for masculine toughness.

But a panel discussion on ESPN's "Outside the Lines" brought in religion. Chris Broussard, an NBA analyst for ESPN and a Christian, was asked what he thought about the specific part of Collins's announcement where he claimed to embrace Christian values and the teaching of Jesus Christ, "particularly the ones that touch on tolerance and understanding."[2] Broussard's response was clear and to the point:

> "Personally I don't believe that you can live an openly homosexual lifestyle or an openly premarital sex between heterosexuals (sic)," Broussard said. "If you're openly living that type of lifestyle, the Bible says you know them by their fruits, it says that's a sin. If you're openly living in unrepentant

sin, whatever it may be, not just homosexuality, adultery, fornication, premarital sex between heterosexuals, whatever it may be. I think that's walking in open rebellion to God and to Jesus Christ. I would not characterize that person as a Christian because I don't think the Bible would characterize them as a Christian."[3]

You can imagine how that went over. Though the statement condemned the sexual behavior of just about every player in the NBA, it was what he said about homosexuality that created the uproar. His clarifying statement later that day did little to calm the angry mob calling for his immediate termination from the network.[4]

At first glance, this incident illustrates how historic Christian teaching about sexuality is treated in the American public square, particularly the media. Though Broussard was asked in a public setting for his personal opinion *as a Christian,* he was expected to have a different one than that historically held by popes, pastors, theologians and a significant number of the American population. The response from pro-LGBT forces whenever this sort of opinion is stated publically is now fully predictable: call it bigotry and demand the violator be silenced in the name of tolerance and acceptance. The same reaction was leveled at Pastor Louis Giglio in 2012 when he was invited by President Obama to pray at his second inauguration. The only difference was that Giglio's guilty comments had been delivered in a sermon some 20 years earlier.

A closer look at the Collins-Broussard incident reveals something much deeper about our culture: Our view of what it means to be human has fundamentally changed. What Christians often see as a cultural *slip* of sexual morality is actually a "cosmological shift" of anthropology. Across Western culture, we are seeing what Rod Dreher has called "Sex After Christianity."[5]

What Is a Human Being?

The common reaction when someone, like Jason Collins for instance, publically "comes out" as gay, lesbian, bi-sexual or transgender, is that they are now able to "be themselves." Because it's "who they are," anything less than full acceptance of their new identification is unthinkable. While some hold outdated opinions based in personal religious view or bigotry, they must be kept private and out of the public square. So, Broussard should not have offered an opinion like that even though he was asked for it. We are all expected to know these new rules that govern our personal opinions.

In 2013, for example, the New Mexico Supreme Court upheld an earlier decision by the state's Human Rights Commission, which found Elane Photography guilty of discrimination. A few years earlier, Elaine Huguenin had refused to photograph a same-sex commitment ceremony. Photographing a gay or lesbian person was one thing, she argued, but photographing a commitment ceremony would amount to endorsing conduct that violated her deeply held convictions. The court rejected her argument, despite the fact that photographers make similar distinctions between a person and a person's conduct all the time (e.g., in cases involving pornography or nudity).

In his concurring opinion, Justice Richard Bosson wrote:

> The Huguenins are free to think, to say, to believe, as they wish; they may pray to the God of their choice and follow those commandments in their personal lives wherever they lead. The Constitution protects the Huguenins in that respect and much more. But there is a price, one that we all have to pay somewhere in our civic life.
>
> In the smaller, more focused world of the marketplace, of commerce, of public accommodation, the Huguenins have to channel their conduct, not their beliefs, so as to leave space for other Americans who believe something different.[6]

According to Bosson, a business owner may hold personal beliefs but must separate those beliefs from their business. And yet, Bosson further wrote, they are not allowed to make a similar distinction between LGBT conduct and an LGBT person. Accepting this blatant inconsistency is, he said, "the price of citizenship."

The lesbian couple, though they quickly found another photographer for their ceremony, was not required to pay this "price of citizenship" or "leave space for other Americans who believe something different." The couple could, in fact, force Huguenin to separate her convictions from her behavior so that they wouldn't have to. Religious convictions are private and personal, but LGBT convictions are "who they are."

In an ironic twist to the story, a gay hair stylist in New Mexico dropped governor Susana Martinez as a client in 2012 because of her opposition to same-sex marriage.[7] The governor didn't file a complaint, so we can only wonder whether the ruling from the Elane Photography case would apply when the shoe is on the other foot.

We'll return to the incredible implications this case carries for religious freedom in a later chapter, but the point we want to consider here is what this reveals about how we now think about human identity. Sexual identity is human identity. Religious identity is not. This is the "cosmological shift" that has taken place in the West.

The historic Western understanding of the human person was that we are fundamentally *religious* creatures. This doesn't mean that everyone in the history of Western civilization agreed on religion or believed in the same religious ideals, but that it was commonly held that *the most important thing about humans is the metaphysical search for the meaning and purpose of life.* For many, this was considered more fundamental to human identity than physical survival or sexual pleasure. In other words, humans were humans because they wrestled with the big, ultimate questions of existence, such as, *Where did everything come from? Why is anything here? Is there a God? What is right and wrong? How do we know?*

Not everyone consciously wrestles with these questions, of course, nor did everyone throughout the history of Western civilization agree on answers. But in their different ways, Greek philosophers, Christian theologians and agnostic skeptics all held that the proper understanding of life and shaping of society begins with this kind of ultimate reflection on the meaning of reality itself. As humans, we want to know who we are and what we are doing here. Some believe in God and others reject Him. Some conclude that there are moral absolutes and others embrace relativism. But, wherever one lands in their journey, people were seen as fundamentally religious, metaphysical creatures first. In this classic Western view of the human person, people were religious creatures first, not sexual ones.

Now back to Jason Collins, Chris Broussard, Justice Bosson, Elaine Huguenin, and American culture. Jason Collins said, "I am a gay man," and everyone celebrated that he could now be himself. Elaine Huguenin said, "I cannot endorse a same-sex commitment ceremony," and was told to keep her views to herself. Broussard was directly asked about his deeply held religious convictions and was then told they don't belong in the public square.

Western civilization has undergone a top to bottom reversal. Today, people are seen as fundamentally sexual creatures, not metaphysical ones. In the new view of the human person, people are sexual creatures first, not religious ones.

Now, every view of sexuality is rooted in metaphysical assumptions about the meaning of life and human identity. But the quest to wrestle with and answer the ultimate questions has been preempted by the conclusion now demanded of everyone up front: *sexuality is who we are*. This new anthropology is taught with a fervor that rivals the most theocratic states. Loyalty to sexual autonomy is demanded of everyone, easily as much as the loyalty once demanded by historic church teaching to restricting sexual behavior. In this new way of seeing things, religious belief is relegated to the realm of the personal and private, but sexual choices are enshrined and considered self-defining.

This shift, from seeing people as fundamentally religious creatures to seeing them as fundamentally sexual creatures, is the fertile ground in which same-sex marriage has flourished. In this brave new world, sexual choice takes precedence over any presumed purpose of marriage. Defining marriage involves de-privileging those sexual relationships once thought to be better than others.

If this analysis is true, the battle over same-sex marriage was decided, in many ways, decades ago. It was. Here's how it happened.

What Happened to Sex?

You've probably heard the maxim "Ideas have *consequences*." This is, of course, true. The consequences, though, are often unintentional and unforeseen. And there's more to ideas than just where they lead.

Ideas also have *histories*. They don't just drop on a group of people from the pages of a book or a professor's lecture notes. Often, the most impactful ideas are the offspring of earlier, less-influential ideas. And ideas have *contexts*. A relatively unimportant idea in one time and place can, in another time and place, change the course of history. The impact of an idea has a lot to do with where it lands. But ideas without people don't change the world, just as people without ideas don't change the world. Only people with ideas change the world. And, so, we can also say that the most important ideas have *champions*.

How the sexual view of human persons conquered Western culture is the story of ideas and their consequences, history, contexts and champions. It is impossible to tell the complete story in this chapter, but we can hit the highlights. We start with Darwin.

Charles Darwin wasn't the first to suggest that all living creatures descended from a common ancestor, but Western culture at the end of the nineteenth century was ready for *Origin of Species*. Science was booming, and organized religion was in decline. After all, in Europe's collective (and selective) memory, religion led to war, but science led to progress. And science was explaining the world in a way religion had not. For many, Darwin's mechanism of natural selection secured the ultimate triumph of science over religion.

Darwin's idea was powerful. Friedrich Nietzsche, writing a few decades later, proclaimed confidently that God was dead. In other words, God was no longer necessary to explain the universe. The West would get along better without Him, he thought.

More important, Darwinism challenged the idea that humans were created in the image of God. Biologically, Darwinism proposed that humans were animals with a conscience. Animals live, mate and reproduce out of instinct, not morality. The implications were clear, and Darwin's ideas were not confined to biology.

One of Christianity's main contributions to the West was in curbing the male sexual appetite left unencumbered in cultures shaped by paganism. The "puritanical anti-sex" reputation of historic Christianity misses the full picture of how significant this contribution was to the development of Western culture. Rod Dreher writes:

> Paul's teachings on sexual purity and marriage were adopted as liberating in the pornographic, sexually exploitive Greco-Roman culture of the time—exploitive especially of slaves and women, whose value to pagan males lay chiefly in their ability to produce children and provide sexual pleasure. Christianity, as articulated by Paul, worked a cultural revolution, restraining and channeling male eros, elevating the status of both women and of the human body, and infusing marriage—and marital sexuality—with love.[8]

Sexual restraint made sense in a world weary of sex with no rules. But rules only made sense in light of the Christian worldview, which proposed a moral order to which humans are responsible, the sacredness of sexuality as created by God, and a universal human dignity shared by males and females alike. Christians didn't always live up to these high ideals, of course, and not all Darwinists rejected Christian morality. But Darwinism helped create an intellectual context that allowed other bad ideas to flourish.[9]

For example, the ground was fertile for Sigmund Freud's idea that sexual repression could account for nearly every psychological disorder, including belief in traditional religion. Sexual ethics grounded in Christianity were, Freud thought, oppressive and should be discarded. New ethics, grounded in reason and science, could be formulated to replace them. Though Freud's psychoanalysis has been largely discredited, his basic take on sexuality remains.

Margaret Sanger, founder of Planned Parenthood, went further. Not only should Christian sexual ethics be replaced, she thought Christianity itself should be replaced with sexual alternatives to heaven and salvation. "Through sex," Sanger wrote, "mankind may attain the great spiritual illumination that will transform the world, which will light up the only path to earthly paradise."[10] For Sanger, birth control was the means of this new salvation, enabling sexual freedom without worry of pregnancy while ridding the world of those she considered to be the "unfit." Sanger's eugenics (which have been whitewashed from Planned Parenthood's website) are undeniable from her writings.

Perhaps most influential was Alfred Kinsey. His book *Sexual Behavior in the Human Male* (also known as *The Kinsey Report*) convinced a culture eager to rid itself of sexual norms that no such norms actually exist. Unencumbered from antiquated ideas about sexual morality, Kinsey thought we should instead look at how humans actually behaved sexually. If any person anywhere does it, it's normal and therefore acceptable.

To travel down this slippery slope even in our imagination is dangerous. We now know that Kinsey, his research team and research subjects travelled all the way down that road and back again in their "experiments." But Kinsey had concluded beforehand that sexual behavior was only considered deviant and criminal because of outdated puritanical traditions. In reality, as Benjamin Wiker writes, *The Kinsey Report* was nothing less than "a thickly disguised attempt to force the world to accept his own unnatural sexuality as natural."[11]

How could such extreme ideas become so influential? Good question. While Kinsey's research did enjoy a measure of public influence, the real explanation for his influence is that his ideas had two champions: an artist and an educator.[12]

The artist was Hugh Hefner. *That's a generous use of the word "artist,"* you may be thinking. True enough. Hefner was not an artist in the same sense as Michelangelo and da Vinci, but he was in the sense that he embodied ideas that captured the cultural imagination. And he was a committed disciple of Alfred Kinsey.

"*Playboy* freed a generation from guilt about sex," Hefner once said, "changed some laws and helped launch a revolution or two. Playboy is the magazine that changed America."[13] It's hard to disagree with this self-assessment. Images that scandalized the public in the early days of *Playboy* were so tame by comparison that they wouldn't make the cover of grocery store tabloids today. And, of course, the Internet has taken the industry launched by *Playboy* to previously unimagined levels. According to one study, 35 percent of all online searches are now pornographic. As journalist Pamela Paul has argued, our culture has officially become "Pornified."[14]

Mary Calderone was the co-founder of the Sexuality Information and Education Council of the United States (SIECUS). While Hefner was bringing Kinsey's ideas about human sexuality into popular culture, Calderone was delivering it directly to children through education. SIECUS, launched from the Kinsey Institute, quickly became "the most influential resource for sex education in America's public schools." And *Playboy* provided its initial funding. "One can only conclude," writes S. Michael Craven, "that *Playboy*'s interest in educating children on sex would be for the furtherance of the Kinsey philosophy and the ultimate cultivation of future *Playboy* consumers."[15]

According to Calderone:

> A new stage of evolution is breaking across the horizon and the task of educators is to prepare children to step into that new world. To do this, they must pry children away from old views and values, especially from biblical and other traditional forms of sexual morality—for religious laws or rules about sex were made on the basis of ignorance.[16]

For Calderone, religious views and values about sex were "ignorant," but *The Kinsey Report* was science.

Many more factors contributed to the cosmological shift than those we've described, including the '60s, the Stonewall riots,

Lawrence v. Texas, the Monica Lewinsky scandal, online pornography, Madonna and Miley Cyrus. But our point here has been to trace the ideas that unseated the traditional view of the human person and replaced them with the sexual view. Once this view dominated the cultural landscape, redefining marriage to include same-sex couples was inevitable.

One additional aspect of this story, however, must not be overlooked. Though same-sex marriage is a fundamental redefinition of the institution, it is not the first, or the only, legal initiative to do so. No-fault divorce laws also fundamentally altered the definition of marriage.

Then California Governor Ronald Reagan signed the first no-fault divorce law in 1969. Within 15 years, nearly every other state had followed suit. Marriage legally became an arrangement one could opt in and out of for whatever reason they wished. Marriage was about being "in love," not fulfilling a life-long commitment to one's spouse and children. As Brad Wilcox writes:

> In this new psychological approach to married life, one's primary obligation was not to one's family but to one's self; hence, marital success was defined not by successfully meeting obligations to one's spouse and children but by a strong sense of subjective happiness in marriage—usually to be found in and through an intense, emotional relationship with one's spouse.[17]

No-fault divorce enshrined a new model of marriage, what Wilcox calls "the soul-mate model," into law. By 1970, the divorce rate had skyrocketed.

As Plato observed, the law is a moral teacher, shaping the boundaries of the cultural imagination. Since 1970, faith in the permanence of marriage has plummeted while the cohabitation rate has dramatically increased. This is particularly true of the nation's underclass.[18]

The incredible personal and social cost of divorce should make us reconsider no-fault divorce laws, but the cat is out of the bag. Most Americans can't even imagine marriage as anything other than the "soul-mate" model. And, if that's all there is to marriage, we ought not to be surprised that same-sex marriage seems so reasonable to so many.

What We Know About Sexual Orientation

AN INTERVIEW WITH KATHY KOCH

We live in an over-sexed culture, and it causes tons of confusion for children. What can parents do to help their children understand sexual wholeness and develop a strong identity as a person?

Children learn who they are by listening to what parents and other significant people in their lives say about them—including things they overhear them say.

Children should get their identity from what God says about them. In order to do this, parents must know what God's Word declares and they must strategically weave these truths into conversation with their children. Praying these truths over children is also very wise.

God's Word is the protection against lies in our culture, media, the news and even from friends who don't know the Scriptures. For our children to be transformed into Christlikeness, the "I Am" statements from the New Testament are key. These statements will develop a strong, complete and accurate identity for children—including sexual wholeness.

What do we know about how sexual identity is formed? What are the myths out there about sexual orientation?

The main myth is that homosexuals are born that way. There is no strong scientific evidence that this is true. Those who believe they are born gay often get mad at God. They say He is supposed to be good—but being gay is a struggle so they ask why God would allow it. Of course, He is good and it's a myth that He doesn't want the best for each of us. Sometimes what is best for us includes challenges—even consistent sin temptations—because He designed us to be refined and strengthened by persevering during challenging times.

A person's background and experiences may cause them to develop confusion about sexuality. Although there may be reasons why people develop and act upon same-sex attraction, that doesn't excuse their sin. An individual is more than a result of his or her experiences, so when two people experience the same circumstances they may not have the same sin temptations. A person's temperament, personality, Mind Style™, passion, developed identity, spiritual maturity and other issues contribute to his or her responses to all of life.

In an environment where attitudes and behaviors support gender stereotypes, the result for some can be sexual identity confusion. For example, my work with hundreds of men with same-sex attraction who have chosen to put Christ first shows that a higher percentage of these men, than in the normal population, highly value their relationships and are stressed when others are upset. They want to be appreciated by others and are sensitive, perceptive, compassionate and spontaneous. When they discover this and see how many straight men have these same preferences, they're deeply relieved to discover they weren't born gay—they were born with strengths that are often rejected as not manly enough. Many reported experiencing painful rejection from straight men and self-rejection, as well. Desperate for male affirmation, many fell sexually and their first homosexual experience was often with a sensitive soul like themselves.

Some believe the myth that when same-sex temptation remains after making a commitment to Christ, these people may not be true believers or they haven't repented or they haven't prayed enough. Those who make these judgments don't use the same standards for themselves and their temptations to overeat, cheat, gossip and be lazy, and that frustrates me. In God's strength, we can change our beliefs and behaviors. He may choose to not change our attractions, but that doesn't make us weak or God weak.

What does unconditional love look like from a family member or friend to someone who is struggling with sexual identity and sexual behavior?

Unconditional love is being there for them, advocating for them to others, protecting them from harm, and effectively and carefully communicating disappointment in their choices. It means not always talking about their sin choices and not acting like we haven't made any.

This love means we treat them consistently no matter the sin. If we wouldn't kick them out for one sexual sin, we don't kick them out for another. If we wouldn't kick them out for a non-sexual sin, we don't kick them out for sexual sin. This love in Christian families means we care more about their spiritual condition than anything else. We trust them into God's loving care and pray rather than worry.

Kathy Koch, Ph.D., is the founder and president of Celebrate Kids, Inc., and is the co-author of *No More Perfect Kids: Love Your Kids for Who They Are* and the author of *How Am I Smart? A Parent's Guide to Multiple Intelligences* (Moody Publishers).

Part 2

What We Can Do
for Marriage

*Bravely take hold of the real, not dallying now with what might be.
Not in the flight of ideas but only in action is freedom. Make up your
mind and come out into the tempest of the living.*

Dietrich Bonhoeffer[1]

This Is No Time for Escape and Christianity Is No Excuse

Somebody (we think it was Plato) said, "Let me write the songs of a nation, and I care not who writes its laws." "Same Love" by Macklemore is a great example. This apologetic for same-sex marriage, delivered with all the musical excellence one would expect from a Vanilla Ice look-a-like contest, earned Macklemore a Grammy for best new artist of 2013. As he performed his hit song during the nationally televised award show, Queen Latifah presided over a wedding ceremony for an intentionally diverse collection of hetero- and homosexual couples. In a church-like setting, they exchanged rings before a serenading choir that featured Madonna and a live audience of tearful witnesses.

Anyone who expected the incident to be as controversial as the Robin Thicke/Miley Cyrus "twerking" incident of a few months earlier was mistaken. That obscene performance at MTV's 2013 Video Music Awards generated cultural noise that lasted weeks, and it made nearly every "year in review" show that December. But within a week of the Grammy Awards, the buzz was gone. It was as if the first same-sex marriage ceremony on national television were a thing expected.

In terms of cultural significance, silence either signifies irrelevance or complete victory. This silence was deafening. Many Christian commentators, us included, spoke and wrote about the ceremony's imagery and implications. We pointed out how same-sex couples were equivocated with interracial couples. We talked about how effectively the arts shape the cultural imagination, and how this strategy had been effectively employed for a national audience. But no one deemed it necessary to respond or disagree. Other than the standard immediate reactions on Twitter, America seemed to extend a disinterested yawn at anyone who still considered same-sex marriage less than normal.

Of course, the debate over same-sex marriage continues. Specific states and various institutions continue to resist. But culturally, and increasingly legally, same-sex marriage is here. The questions to be answered by those of us committed to uphold natural marriage is, What do we do now? How can we be faithful to God's design for marriage in a culture that considers it outdated, hateful and repressive?

In light of our new cultural reality, we continue to hear many of our Christian brothers and sisters conclude, "It's all over." Though not always clear what the "it" is, they typically mean this in one of two ways.

One group proclaims confidently (and happily) that it's the "culture wars" that are over. We tried to change the culture, especially through politics, but we've lost. The lesson to be learned, according to these Christians, is that we've been in the wrong business for too long. It's time to abandon the *culture changing* business (especially when it comes to this issue) and get back to the *people loving* business. Even if we personally believe that same-sex marriage is wrong, they say, it's time to stop trying to change laws and go back to changing hearts.

The other group is far more cynical. For them, cultural efforts are futile and instead we should wait for God's judgment, which most certainly will fall soon. "We" tried to warn "them," but "they" didn't listen. So, "they" (not us) are now going to get what "they" deserve. "We" must protect our families, and ourselves. The only cultural task that remains is to shake our heads and wag our fingers at everyone else. Perhaps the motive is anger, or perhaps a desire for safety, but the result is the same: give up on our culture.

We disagree with each of these approaches. In fact, we think the current cultural situation, including this particular issue of same-sex marriage, brings incredible opportunities for Christians to be "salt and light" in our times. With an informed and winsome boldness, we can continue to stand for marriage while being gentle and loving to those outside of Christ. We'll offer specific ideas in the chapters to come, but in this chapter, we argue that Christians *can* be faithfully engaged in this culture. In fact, we *must*.

Called *to* the World, Not *from* It

Let's start here: This world is a fallen place, but it's not a bad place. These are two very different things. If the world were a bad place, either by design or because our sin made it bad, then the wisest course would be to stay away from it in every way possible. That's what the Gnostics believed. The earliest and most persistent heresy to infect the Church, Gnosticism in its various forms taught that the physical world is evil and that only the spiritual world is good.

But the Bible teaches differently. The Bible describes the world as "good" from God's hand before it describes it as fallen from human hands. And, though fallen, the creation continues to proclaim God's grandeur, kindness and goodness (e.g., Psalm 19:1-2). God intended humans to care for His world, and it remains a place where God's people can make a difference. "When the righteous increase, the people rejoice, but when the wicked rule, the people groan," Proverbs 29:2 tells us. Even while exiled to a pagan land, God instructed Israel through the prophet Jeremiah:

> Build houses and live in them; plant gardens and eat their produce. Take wives and have sons and daughters; take wives for your sons, and give your daughters in marriage, that they may bear sons and daughters; multiply there, and do not decrease. But seek the welfare of the city where I have sent you into exile, and pray to the LORD on its behalf, for in its welfare you will find your welfare (Jeremiah 29:5-7).

For the Christian, living in this good-yet-fallen place means living in tension. The world is profoundly good, yet full of sin and corruption. People have profound capacity for justice, kindness and love even while having profound capacity for injustice, cruelty and hate. Nazi officials sent Jewish children to die in the gas chambers of Auschwitz during the day and then hugged their own children at night.

We may want to avoid this tension, but we cannot. The impulse to flee from culture, even for noble causes like staying away from evil or preserving the relevance of the gospel, tempts the Church in every generation. It's especially appealing for American Christians today, considering what's been lost.

For quite some time, Christianity enjoyed influence and acceptance in Western culture. But by the middle of the twentieth century, writers like Francis Schaeffer, C. S. Lewis and Leslie Newbigin were pointing to clear indicators that the West was becoming "post-Christian." Christianity was being demoted, you might say.

Losing influence is one thing, but losing acceptance is another. It's disappointing when Christian morality is seen as quaint, outdated and wrong. It's painful when it is considered bigoted, hateful and evil.

In this new state of affairs, staying away from the world can seem like the best option. It is certainly easier. Shouldn't we withdraw into the safety of the Church, take care of our own, and avoid the darkness? Won't staying quiet on controversial issues allow us to keep the focus on God's love for *all* people?

This route of escapist safety is just wrong. Christianity is not an escapist religion. To be Christian is to be called into the world, not out of it.

Most religions are escapist. For example, through meditation, moderation and contentment, Buddhism calls its adherents to escape desire and pursue a place of mental peace. Buddhism calls people out of the world.[1]

Hinduism is also escapist. Faithful Hindus seek escape from the physical world (which they consider to be illusory anyway) through a series of births and rebirths. Ultimately, they believe their human identity will be absorbed into the spiritual fabric of the universe.

Oprah-ism is also escapist. America's most popular religion, a syncretistic New Agey sort of spiritual self-helpism, teaches us to follow our hearts and focus on the good in order to escape stress and self-doubt. Looking inward and denying the reality around us, we can become our true happy selves (or something like that).

The center of Christianity, however, is Jesus Christ, the God who put on skin and "moved into our neighborhood" (John 1:14, *THE MESSAGE*). The Christian faith is *incarnational*. God did not merely send a prophet, an angel or a book to solve the world's problems. He came Himself. God, in Jesus Christ, made Himself fully present in the world He made. We must follow His lead.

The incarnation establishes the trajectory of Christian faith. Christianity is no "Let's get out of here so we can stay safe from the evil world until God takes us out of here" sort of religion. Christianity is a faith for the here and now. And the final prayer Jesus prayed for His people on the night before the crucifixion, recorded in John 17, affirms this.

In the Garden of Gethsemane, Jesus specifically prayed for His disciples whom, He said, the world would hate: "I do not ask that you take them out of the world, but that you keep them from the evil one" (v. 15). Jesus wanted them present in the world yet undefiled; in the world, but not of it.

In the larger context of the total prayer, it's clear that being in the world is not just a necessary evil to be endured. Rather, it is a means by which their faith would grow. Jesus' greatest desire for His disciples, which He expresses at the beginning of the prayer, was "that they may know you, the only true God and Jesus Christ whom you have sent" (v. 3). Knowing Jesus happens not by escaping the world but by living in it.

This applies to believers throughout history also. "I pray not only for these," Jesus said, "but for all those who will believe in me because of their word" (v. 18). What Jesus prayed for His disciples, He prays for all believers.

Writing from Tegel prison on July 21, 1944, Dietrich Bonhoeffer described how he had come to this understanding of faith:

> During the last year or so, I've come to know and understand more and more the profound this-worldliness of Christianity. The Christian is not a *homo religiosus,* but simply a man, as Jesus was a man . . . I don't mean the shallow and banal this-worldliness of the enlightened, the busy, the comfortable, or the lascivious, but the profound this-worldliness, characterized by discipline and the constant knowledge of death and resurrection . . . I thought that I could acquire faith by trying to live a holy life or something like that. . . I discovered later, and I'm still discovering right up to this moment, that it is only by living completely in this world that one learns to have faith.[2]

Incredibly, just one day earlier, the final attempt to assassinate Adolf Hitler had failed and the conspiracy had been revealed.

The "this moment" that Bonhoeffer referred to was the moment he knew his role in the conspiracy would be discovered, and he would likely never return to his family and fiancée.[3]

Still, Bonhoeffer believed that his long and disappointing journey had revealed to him what Christian faith truly was. Real Christianity means boots on the ground. The call to the Christian, following in the steps of Jesus Christ, is *to* the world not away from it.

Called to Our Times, Not Another

Not only are we called to the world; we are called to our particular culture. Acts 17 describes Paul's interaction with Epicurean and Stoic philosophers in the intellectual center of Athens. There on Mars Hill, Paul described the one true God to a group of people who, though "very religious," knew nothing of Jesus Christ:

> The God who made the world and everything in it, being Lord of heaven and earth, does not live in temples made by man, nor is he served by human hands, as though he needed anything, since he himself gives to all mankind life and breath and everything. And he made from one man every nation of mankind to live on all the face of the earth, *having determined allotted periods and the boundaries of their dwelling place*, that they should seek God, and perhaps feel their way toward him and find him. Yet he is actually not far from each one of us (Acts 17:24-27, emphasis added).[4]

According to Paul, God establishes the time and place in which all people live. We may wish for another culture for ourselves or for our families, but it's no accident we are in *this* time and place. God ordained it.

So, we really *can't* escape culture. If we work, shop, travel, play, eat out, watch, listen or otherwise leave our homes, we encounter culture. And so do our children.

One morning at breakfast, my (John's) wife turned on the worship song "Bless the Lord, O My Soul." My five-year-old daughter asked, "Mommy, is that Justin Bieber?" I assure you that no Justin Bieber song has ever played in our home and, if I have my way, never will. Justin Bieber has never even been a topic of conversation in our home. How did my daughter even know his name?

That's the power of culture. We can't escape it. That's why it was so confusing, and even a little infuriating, to hear that a youth pastor of a very large and influential church proclaimed to one of our friends, "I'm done talking about same-sex marriage. That ship has sailed." What on earth could that possibly mean? Living in America today ensures that you *must* talk about it. It's part of our culture. The kids in that youth group will grow up, fall in love and watch their friends, family and neighbors do the same. Who will they fall in love with? How should they act on their feelings? What if they wish to act on their own same-sex attraction? What if there is a same-sex wedding on national television? (Oh wait, that already happened.) To not offer any guidance on same-sex marriage to the next generation is a dereliction of duty.

The truth is, cultural escape is impossible. Like it or not, we'll just have to move forward and figure out together how to navigate the reality of same-sex marriage with all of its implications. And we'll have to faithfully pursue God's intention for marriage whether or not Hollywood, the Supreme Court, Macklemore or our relatives and neighbors will, in the end, agree.

Final Thoughts: Two Reminders and Three Questions

As we move on in the next chapters to specifics, let's keep three things in mind. First, we aren't the first Christians to face a difficult culture nor will we be the last. And it could be worse. John the Baptist lost his head for proclaiming God's view of marriage to King Herod (see Matthew 14:1-12). Believers throughout history were forced to flee for their lives after speaking truth to power. Depressed and disillusioned after the great victory over the prophets of Baal, the prophet Elijah thought he was alone (see 1 Kings 18-19). But he wasn't, and neither are we. We run the race surrounded by a "great cloud of witnesses" of those who have gone before (Hebrews 11:12). In doing so, we join them. It's good company in which to be.

Second, we need to remember that culture is influenced as much from the middle as it is from the top down. American culture is diverse and multi-faceted, but the 24-hour news cycle locks our attention on Washington, D.C., New York City and Hollywood. These centers of cultural power matter. We are thankful that God calls Christians to those places, but for all that is forced on us by cultural elites, all of us are called to steward our own communities. This is what we mean by the "middle" of culture: families, churches, community groups, Little League and city councils are within reach of most of us and within the scope of our responsibility. Let's be faithful and hopeful wherever we can, instead of only looking in despair at the top of culture.

The impact of these "middle" institutions is significant. Among the gravest threats to religious liberty are locally passed statutes, not just federal laws. The next generation is more influenced by their parents and peers than by celebrities and executive orders. Whatever we can do, let's do it.

Third, there's far more to concern us than same-sex marriage. If a sweeping federal law were passed tomorrow that defined marriage as between one man and one woman, the institution of marriage would still be in dreadful shape. Plus, there would still be unwanted children, systemically poor neighborhoods, abortions, predatory pornography, inner-city violence, school failures and spousal abuse. Plenty of culturally significant work remains for the Church in every time and in every place. Our time and place are no exception.

Our responsibility is bigger than merely fighting against same-sex marriage; our responsibility is to fight *for* marriage. Same-sex marriage is a *fruit*, not the *root*. It's a cultural signpost that indicates just how far we've journeyed away from God's intent for sex and marriage. Yes, we should stop as soon as we can, but we also need to turn around and head in the right direction.

For too long, many assumed that marriage would be protected by popular vote. "Every time it goes to the polls," they'd say, "the people protect one-man/one-woman marriage." It's all too clear now that this was merely a short-term observation, not a long-term strategy.

Now, others are trying to protect marriage through other forms of political leverage, like the courts or a Constitutional Amendment. Every legitimate option should be explored, but two things should be remembered. First, there is no silver bullet that will stop same-sex marriage. Court decisions and political victories cannot withstand cultural tsunamis. As it is already, particularly with younger generations, we've lost a lot of momentum. Second, political power is a fickle friend. If you win an issue this way, you can lose it this way. Just ask the prohibitionists of the early twentieth century.[5]

In light of this reality, Christians should shift their mindset from *preserving* or *conserving* to *proposing* and *building*. Christians should no longer wish for a massive judicial or political victory to save marriage. When an institution has been culturally compromised the way marriage has been, it cannot be saved. It has to be redefined and reestablished.

It's an enormous task, of course. But we aren't the first Christians to propose a biblical marriage ethic to a sexually licentious culture. Christians blessed pagan Rome, pre-Victorian England and various tribal cultures throughout history with the life-giving view of sex and marriage Scripture describes. Love for God and love for neighbor demand that we seek to bless our culture as well.

This won't be easy, of course. And it's difficult to know where to begin. These three questions can guide our engagement in a gospel-centered way:

1. *What's good around me that I can promote, preserve and protect?* Wherever we can demonstrate that marriage is good for our communities, let's do it. Whenever we can celebrate the beauty of life-long married love, and however we can protect our own homes, and pursue holiness and peace in our communities, we should. The Church must *champion* marriage. And it begins with each of us. We must be willing to ask, "Does my life reflect the biblical definition of marriage and family?"

2. *What's evil around me that I can stop?* If pornography is coming into our homes, we must stop it. If bad relational habits infect our own marital unions, let's break them. The Church must continue to unseat the bad ideas about love, sex and marriage that are victimizing people in our culture, especially women and children. The Church must *defend* marriage from all that is attacking it.

3. *What's broken around me that I can help restore, renew or reconcile?* Communities torn apart by fractured relationships need to see the gospel in action. Christ reconciles broken relationships, vertically and horizontally. This hope extends to those who struggle with same-sex attraction, opposite-sex attraction, sexual addiction, divorce and abuse. And hope remains because Christ has risen from the dead. The Church must become a force to *restore* relationships.

What we are up against is formidable. Speaking and living the gospel in the days to come could cost us dearly. It could also provide the greatest opportunity for the Church to be the Church in our generation. Most likely, it will be both.

What Same-Sex Marriage Means for the Church's Role in Culture

An Interview with Eric Teetsel

In what ways have defenders of natural marriage misunderstood the issue of same-sex marriage? What have we missed?

The issue of same-sex marriage is a symptom of a much larger contest over meaning, truth and—indeed—the very nature of God. Most of us who work with this issue understand these bigger questions and the significance of same-sex marriage as an inflection point leading us closer to or farther from God's best plan for the world. Our position is necessary, but there is a downside. We often forget that the vast majority of our fellow citizens who identify as homosexuals are not part of a decades-old conspiracy to undermine the foundation of civilization; they are everyday people with jobs, hobbies, family and to-do lists. What they want may be wrong and more harmful than they know, but our tendency to overlook their humanity has hampered our ability to communicate with them effectively and to convey the love of Christ.

Some argue that same-sex marriage is inevitable, and therefore Christians should just move on from this debate. Do you agree? Why or why not?

America is nearing a stasis in the legislative battle for state-by-state same-sex marriage (SSM) recognition. States where the population wants SSM have granted it, and those that don't have rejected attempts to legislate it into existence. If not for the courts, things would likely stay this way for the foreseeable future. However, any one of the many lawsuits working their way through the courts could potentially thrust SSM on the nation. So, yes, in a sense same-sex marriage seems inevitable because of unjust judicial overreach.

Does this mean Christians should move on? Absolutely not. Just as the Church has led the fight against abortion with increasing success, our witness will be required in a long-term fight for the truth and good of marriage.

*What are the most important things Christians can do
for marriage in today's culture?*

The Manhattan Declaration provides the answer: "To strengthen families, we must stop glamorizing promiscuity and infidelity and restore among our people a sense of the profound beauty, mystery, and holiness of faithful marital love. We must reform ill-advised policies that contribute to the weakening of the institution of marriage, including the discredited idea of unilateral divorce. We must work in the legal, cultural, and religious domains to instill in young people a sound understanding of what marriage is, what it requires, and why it is worth the commitment and sacrifices that faithful spouses make."[6]

Eric Teetsel directs the Manhattan Declaration, a national movement of Christians for life, marriage and religious freedom founded by Charles Colson.

8

Learning from the Past: A Movement Worth Examining

Riding the wake of the sexual revolution, the "gay liberation" movement secured accommodation and, in many ways, privileged status for gays and lesbians in the midst of a hostile cultural environment. By almost every measure, it is the most successful social movement in recent memory, changing not only many hearts and minds but also more than a few laws and institutions.

Shifting a culture isn't an easy thing to do, but this movement did it. It's instructive to know both what they were able to change and how they did it. If we hope to shift culture in a pro-marriage way, this is a story we should know.

What Is a Movement?

A "movement" is difficult to define.[1] It takes more than a group of people buying into the same agenda, joining a formal organization or following a charismatic leader. Opponents often see members of a movement as a homogenous group, but often, members do not trust or like each other, and at times, are not aware they are part of a movement. There typically isn't a "secret playbook," though movements can be mobilized by manifestos and calls to action. And, contrary to what is commonly thought, movements are not created by cultural elites forcing an agenda down the throats of the public (though, admittedly, the gay movement has enjoyed significant help from national media and the courts).

Movements prove that multiple groups working from multiple angles for a common cause can generate tremendous social change. Embarrassing failures and unexpected successes yield important lessons, and if groups learn the strategic leverage points of cultural influence, they can change things even if they find themselves outside the typical cultural power centers. The gay movement is a prime example.

After the Ball: The Gay Movement

> We, the people, declare today that the most evident of truths—that all of us are created equal—is the star that guides us still, just as it guided our forebears through Seneca Falls, and Selma and Stonewall, just as it guided all those men and women, sung and unsung, who left footprints along this great Mall, to hear a preacher say that we cannot walk alone, to hear a King proclaim that our individual freedom is inextricably bound to the freedom of every soul on Earth.[2]

In his second inaugural address, President Barack Obama formally connected three causes. The Stonewall Riot of 1969 is remembered as a defining moment for the gay movement, much like the Selma March is for the Civil Rights Movement, and the Seneca Falls Convention is for the Woman's Rights Movement. On June 28 of that year, police raided the Stonewell Inn, a popular gay bar in Greenwich Village, and "a handful of long-suffering New York drag queens, tired of homophobic police harassment picked up rocks and bottles and fought back."[3] A few days later, *The Village Voice* proclaimed, "(gay) liberation is under way."[4]

But 20 years after Stonewall, Marshal Kirk and Hunter Madsen grimly concluded, "The gay revolution has failed."[5] In their book *After the Ball: How America Will Conquer Its Fear and Hatred of Gays in the '90s*, these authors claimed that "practically everything so far done by gays to better their lot, though done with honesty and dedication, has been done incorrectly."[6] Ouch! But they did more than bluntly point out mistakes; they offered a new way forward. Theirs was a savvy and subversive game plan, and it worked.

Though many gay activists did not appreciate the criticism at the time, and many in the LGBT community today have never heard of *After the Ball*, it's a mistake to underestimate its importance. The midstream correction it offered came at a time when success was very much in doubt, and it is a primary reason the 25 years since *After the Ball* have been so different than the 20 before it.

The movement succeeded because it became smarter. Kirk and Madsen realized the "we're here, we're queer, get used to it" methods of gay activists would never accomplish the sort of full and unqualified acceptance they were demanding. Most Americans at the time found homosexuality distasteful; so *After the Ball* proposed a more modest, yet more strategic goal: Americans must learn to see homosexuality as another, normal way to live life. Why waste time trying to convince America to *like* homosexuality? It was good enough for them to not *dislike* it. "In brief," Kirk and Madsen clarified, "we're fighting for a tomorrow in which it simply doesn't occur to anyone that there's anything more unusual about being gay than about preferring praline ice cream to double Dutch chocolate . . ."[7]

Change They Could Believe In

The gay movement already believed America needed to change, but *After the Ball* clarified which changes to pursue. The major obstacle facing the gay movement, Kirk and Madsen thought, was that straight Americans were *unfamiliar* with gays and gayness. They knew very little about gays, were convinced there weren't that many to begin with anyway (certainly no one they knew), and felt no obligation to fight on their behalf.

Straights were not only unfamiliar with gays, Kirk and Madsen continued; they were *misinformed*. Their impressions came from the flamboyant caricatures portrayed by media and, too often, by gays themselves. Many believed homosexuality was a mental disorder or, even worse, a sinful lifestyle chosen by sex addicts inflamed by lust. As long as the "limp-wristed," feminized gay man or "male-hating," homely lesbian stereotypes persisted, straight America would never see gays as productive members of society and would never come to their defense.[8]

Therefore, Kirk and Madsen concluded, America must be reeducated to believe that gays are a significant minority of every community who positively contribute like everyone else. Most important, they must be taught that gays don't choose their feelings or attractions any more than heterosexuals do, and that their love is just as sincere and valid.

Changing these beliefs would breed better treatment of gays, but the authors did not wish to leave this to chance. Their goals were clear. All legal restrictions on sexual behavior between consenting adults, especially anti-sodomy laws, had to be dismantled. All discrimination against gays must be made illegal instead, including "all efforts to keep gays from speaking, fraternizing, organizing, working in the jobs and residing in the neighborhoods they would choose, marrying and acquiring property together, and parenting children."[9] And vocal disapproval of gays was to be removed from the public square.[10]

How It Could Happen

On this side of history, it's easy to miss just how ambitious this agenda was at the time. Kirk and Madsen proposed nothing less than an entire overhaul of culture! And they had a three-step plan to get there.

First, we *desensitize* the American public. "Inundate them," the authors wrote, "in a continuous flood of gay-related advertising, presented in the least offensive fashion possible."[11] Second, *jam* anti-gay bigotry with competing emotions like shame, sympathy or empathy. Bigotry could not be argued away, they realized, but the bigot could be made into the bad guy "without reference to facts, logic or proof."[12] Finally, *convert* the public. A converted America would see no difference between gays and straights. "We mean," the authors clarified, "conversion of the average American's emotions, mind and will, through a planned psychological attack, in the form of propaganda fed to the nation via the media."[13]

So there you have it: focused goals, defined success, and a preferred vehicle (media). But there was more. The authors realized that the gay movement's success depended as much on the how as the what. So they offered eight principles of persuasion to guide the process.

First, they said, gays had to improve their communication skills. Gays were eager to "self-express" but not willing to consider where the American public stood on the issue. They wanted to preach, but no one was listening. That had to change.

Second, the plan should target "skeptics." It's both impossible and unnecessary to change the minds of everyone. Haters would always be haters, the authors concluded, but most Americans could be emotionally converted to either advocacy or to silence. Either one would do.

Third, they suggested, "Talk about gayness until the issue becomes thoroughly tiresome."[14] But, they quickly added, America wasn't ready for talk about gay *behavior*. Gay rights and discrimination were the topics that would "muddy the moral waters" and neutralize "religious bigotry."[15]

Fourth, they said, stay focused and on topic. Taking on other social justice causes would only compromise their effectiveness.

Fifth, portray gays as victims of both circumstance (i.e., they didn't choose their identity) and discrimination (i.e., bigots were the "aggressors"). This would disrupt the "gays are after your children" narrative. Even better, it would turn some straights into protectors.

Sixth, potential protectors needed a cause. Straights needed to know where and how to defend victims of discrimination. They needed to be called to action.

Seventh, "make gays look good."[16] Counter the unhelpful stereotypes, often perpetuated by gays themselves, with a different image. Dead heroes and live celebrities were most promising, they suggested.

Finally, the authors suggested, connect those who oppose gays with the villains of history. After all, no one defends anti-Semites and Klansmen. The social cost should be high enough to dissuade people from resisting change.

By now you may be thinking, *This all sounds familiar*. And it should. The *After the Ball* plan also included sample advertisements, strategies for specific media forms, and many more concrete examples of how their suggestions could be creatively implemented. Many were implemented. And, for the most part, they worked.

Lessons to Be Learned

Can Christians really learn from *After the Ball*? Absolutely. Not only can we learn how the gay movement accomplished most of its goals in less than a generation, captured the moral high ground, and made it difficult to defend natural marriage, but we can also learn how cultures can be influenced and changed.

First, *passionate conviction is not enough. After the Ball* clarified the gay movement's passion. Clarity saves a lot of wasted energy, anger and effort. Without it, a movement won't succeed.

In a culture with such a poor understanding of marriage, we need clear targets. For example, the wrong idea that marriage exists only to further personal happiness and mutual affection must be uprooted and replaced. The notion that feelings or impulses determine our identity and justify our behavior is insidious and dangerous. The idea that marriage should serve our sexual choices, rather than the other way around, and that gender is irrelevant must be targeted too.

Marriage must be both taught and portrayed as an institution that is bigger than our desires, whims, feelings and affections. And, before we start jumping on our soapboxes, we have our own houses (and thinking) to clean up. We cannot assume that those in the Church understand the real purpose of marriage any more than those outside of it. So, a primary community to target for this change of thought (and heart) is *us*, not *them*.

Second, *After the Ball* proves that *having a message is not enough*. Communication requires an audience. "Speaking from the heart" without knowing where the audience stands is ineffective and can even be damaging. Kirk and Madsen pressed the gay movement to cater their message to what their audience was prepared to hear, instead of just repeating everything they wanted to say. A message is only effective if it can be heard.

We work with thousands of students each year. Most have no idea what a phrase like "let's preserve traditional marriage" even means. Many have never seen a traditional marriage (or even a television show with a traditional marriage), and the marriages they see are not worth defending. Plus, professors and media incessantly proclaim to them how traditional marriage oppresses women, discriminates against gays and lesbians, and limits personal freedom. *Why preserve something that wasn't good in the beginning?* they think. Better to redefine marriage so that more people can be happy or stay silent and safe.

We ought not assume that our audience, inside or outside the Church, understands what natural marriage is or how it is good for everyone. Attacking same-sex marriage sounds like bigotry to those who don't understand natural marriage. Knowing this doesn't change our message, but it must change how we deliver our message.

We also must expect to be asked questions about same-sex marriage, whether at work or across the Thanksgiving table or on national media. We should be ready. And when asked, we ought not expect a level playing field.

When *What Is Marriage? Man and Woman: A Defense* co-author Ryan Anderson was invited to have a "conversation" with Suze Orman on *Piers Morgan Live* in March 2013, he experienced firsthand the second-class status imposed on those who publically defend natural marriage. Not only did he face Orman, but he also faced a condescending host and a hostile crowd. He was refused a place on the stage with Orman and Morgan, and was instead forced to sit in the crowd.[17]

Despite how he was treated, Anderson modeled a calm, cool approach. He was kind and did not reciprocate when called "uneducated" and "not American." (Anderson has a graduate degree from Princeton and is in a Ph.D. program at Notre Dame.) He was clearly prepared.

As well as Anderson did in that hostile environment, the whole bizarre episode revealed that when it comes to this emotionally charged issue, arguments only go so far. And so a third lesson we can glean from *After the Ball* is that *a good argument is no match for a compelling story.*

Kirk and Madsen understood that their movement could win the battle of ideas through the imagination, not arguments. People are moved more by emotion than conviction, they realized. As Eric Teetsel of the Manhattan Declaration says, "The gay movement realized a long time ago that the battle over culture wasn't a boxing match of ideas, but a beauty pageant with 300 million judges." A boxer rarely wins on looks.

We have powerful stories, too, of life-long married love and sacrificial commitment. There are redemptive stories of those who found in Christ an identity deeper and more substantial than their sexuality. There are difficult stories of victims of the failing marriage culture. Too often, any stories that counter the culturally accepted narrative about homosexual or transgender acceptance are suppressed. But the stories must be told. The truth and the lives they represent matter.

As important as these lessons are, Christians cannot just reverse and repeat the plan from *After the Ball*. Some of their strategies are out of bounds for followers of Jesus Christ. The end we seek is noble, but it does not justify the following means:

1. Passionate conviction is no excuse for dishonesty.

In several places, Kirk and Madsen imply that lying is justified as long as it serves the cause. For example, they admit that sexual orientation is shaped by both nature and nurture, but they instructed gays to promote the "born that way" narrative in order to reinforce that gays are victims. Even if it's not completely true, they suggest, it's useful. Also, though an advertisement may wrongly portray the gay experience or an opponent's motive, they say, "It makes no difference that the ads are lies; not to us, because we're using them to ethically good effect, to counter negative stereotypes that are every bit as much as lies, and far more wicked ones."[18]

Christians, of course, should not lie, even if for a good cause. Winning a court case, an argument or a culture is never an excuse for being less than truthful. For example, telling stories either too soon or too rosily of men and women who have been "healed" from same-sex attraction, without full disclosure of ongoing struggles, only harms the public message of the gospel in the long run. And it's bearing false witness.

2. Disagreeing is no excuse for demonizing.

In *After the Ball*, there are good guys and bad guys. The good guys are gays and gay advocates, and the bad guys are anyone who disagrees in any way and for any reason. Little distinction is made between gay bashers and those who oppose any part of the agenda.

Christians can be guilty of that too. Painting all gays as pedophiles or sex addicts isn't charitable or honest. For the Christian, people are never enemies. "We do not wrestle against flesh and blood," Paul instructs, "but against the rulers, against the authorities, against the cosmic powers over this present darkness, against the spiritual forces of evil in the heavenly places" (Ephesians 6:12).

Biblically, there are no good guys and bad guys. Everyone is both. All are made in God's image, and all "have sinned" (see Genesis 1:2; Romans 3). Some are in rebellion, and others have repented of their rebellion (see 1 Corinthians 6). Some are living according to God's design, and others are living against it (see Psalm 1). Ultimately, however, we are against homosexual acts and same-sex marriage because we are *for* people. We say no because God does, and He says no because He offers a much better yes.[19]

3. Telling stories doesn't change our responsibility to present good arguments.

We don't have to choose between appealing to emotion and presenting arguments. In fact, we can't choose between the two as Christians. Truth must, at times, be spoken.

Jesus told many memorable stories to persuade people, such as the Prodigal Son, the Good Samaritan, and the Parable of the Sower. But He also quite often *reasoned* with people to persuade them. See, for example, the extensive arguments He presents to the religious leaders in John 6-8.

The controversy risked by argument leads some to give up on proclaimed Christianity altogether. "Remember what St. Francis of Assisi said?" they say. "'Preach the gospel at all times. When necessary, use words.'" We aren't sure who first attributed those words to St Francis, but it is unlikely he ever said them. And, though our actions should match our words, they should not replace them. After all, our Lord is called "the Word." Christianity is a *proclaimed* faith. At times, words are very necessary.[20]

A Final Lesson

One more observation from *After the Ball* is worth our attention. Kirk and Madsen, while railing at the homo-hating culture they perceived all around them, laid plenty of blame on the promiscuity, flamboyance and criminal behavior within the gay movement itself. And they called for change.

Shouldn't Christians be even more willing to look in the mirror and honestly acknowledge our own failings about sex and marriage? After all, we have contributed to the problem. In the next chapter, we turn our attention inward.

First Things First: The Call to Repentance

Marshall Kirk and Hunter Madsen aimed their most stinging indictment at the movement they hoped to mobilize. In the final pages of *After the Ball,* they wrote, "For twenty immature years, the gay community has shrieked for rights while demonstrating an alarming degree of irresponsibility. If gays expect straights ever to accord them their rights, this is one of the things that must change. *We must cease to be our own worst enemies.*"[1]

Twenty-five years later, the tables are turned. Christians face the prospect, particularly on this issue, of being the cultural *persona non grata.* Even common sense defenses of conscience rights, like not forcing bakers or photographers to participate in same-sex wedding ceremonies against their convictions, have been rejected. The initial call for tolerance has become a demand for compliance.

As Ross Douthat wrote in the *New York Times* in response to the defeat of a series of proposed state-level conscience legislation, ". . . such bills have been seen, in the past, as a way for religious conservatives to negotiate surrender—to accept same-sex marriage's inevitability while carving out protections for dissent. But now, apparently, the official line is that *you bigots don't get to negotiate anymore.*"[2] Gloomily, he concluded, "We are not really having an argument about same-sex marriage anymore . . . and we're not having a negotiation. Instead, all that's left is the timing of the final victory—and for the defeated to find out what settlement the victors will impose."[3]

You can guess who he thinks are the winners and losers. Anyone who believes in one-man/one-woman marriage faces a tough state of affairs. Same-sex marriage advocates are enjoying the spoils of victory.

If, in response, we spend the next 20 years pointing out discrimination and lost religious freedoms to the world *without addressing concerns in our own community*, we will become our own worst enemies. It's time to take a long, hard look inward, admit our shortcomings and ask forgiveness from God, from each other and, where appropriate, from the gay community. There is no path forward to building a strong marriage culture that does not begin with a revival of God's people to His design for marriage.

To be clear, religious freedom is in great peril and deserves our attention and protection. But many Christians are so *angry* with the gay community for things both real and perceived that they are not willing to share responsibility for the conditions that made it possible in the first place. We, however, are not innocent. In more ways than we care to admit, Christians helped same-sex marriage happen.

We know some will find that statement offensive, but remember, our own worldview teaches that what's wrong with the world is not just something "out there." Sin is also "in here." Every other worldview claims otherwise. "It's the government's fault," say the anarchists. "It's the wealthy capitalist's fault," say the communists. "It's the inferior's fault," say the racists. "It's the culturally powerfuls' fault," say the postmodernists. But Christians realize the problem is as much *internal* as it is external. As G. K. Chesterton purportedly responded to a London newspaper:

> Dear Sir:
> Regarding your article,
> "What's Wrong with the World?"
> I am.
> Yours Truly,
> G. K. Chesterton[4]

Cleaning Up Our Own Homes First

The main point of this chapter could easily be misconstrued. We are not Church haters, nor are we trying to point out the specks in every other Christian eye but ours. We love the Church. We believe in the Church. We *are* the Church, along with all who are in Christ.

We pray for its success and mourn its failures, and we share in both. In this chapter, we write as *inside participants*, not *outside critics*.

Change comes on the inside before the outside. Paul, in the book of 1 Corinthians, was writing to a church located in a city known for debauchery. Yet, he tells them that they must first confront the grievous sexual sin that is taking place in the church. Redirecting their attention, he asked rhetorically, "For what have I to do with judging outsiders? Is it not those inside the church whom you are to judge? God judges those outside" (1 Corinthians 5:12-13).

The application today is that as Christians, we must spend more energy getting our own houses in order than we do trying to correct those outside the Church. Those in Christ are continually to call each other back to His authority in all areas. Theologian T. M. Moore puts it bluntly:

> The Lord opposes His people from time to time, subjecting them to oppression, futility, division, want and other forms of distress. He does this in order to bring them back to the path of righteousness (Hebrews 12:3-11). When such situations arise, or whenever the people of God find themselves to be in distress, they must first look to themselves, and not to the world, for the cause and thus the remedy of their ills. Our concern must be to discover, not how we may relieve the pressure against or upon us from outside sources, but where we have strayed from the Lord's agenda and purpose. The way out of distress is not, in the first instance, via political change, but by repentance, leading to revival and renewal. We will spend our energies and resources in vain if we think we can bypass repentance in order to secure what we consider to be our rights or freedoms or blessings.[5]

But we are not advocating cultural silence on this issue either. Rather, we must embrace a different tone and a different strategy when appealing to the larger culture. To those outside of Christ, as Chuck Colson wrote, "Christianity does not seek to impose, it proposes."[6]

Also, we are not implying that each and every believer has failed and is therefore personally responsible for the decaying cultural morals of our age. Many heroically live out and champion biblical chastity and marital faithfulness. Many have mastered the difficult task of speaking truth in love. Many have found redemption from past sins and hurts, and now walk in a new way because of Christ. We are so thankful for our parents, for example, who faithfully modeled godly marriage to us. We owe them a tremendous debt.

But it's important to remember that the Scriptures speak corporately to God's people even more than they speak to us personally. All of the New Testament letters, except for four (Titus, Philemon, and 1 and 2 Timothy), were written to churches, not individuals. And think, for example, of Nehemiah's quest to restore Israel's dignity, worship and defenses after their captivity in Babylon. When he learned that the walls of Jerusalem were in disrepair and the remaining Israelites were "in great trouble and shame," he courageously took his concern to the king of Persia. But first, he "sat down and wept and mourned for days, and [he] continued fasting and praying before the God of heaven" (Nehemiah 1:4). *What* he prayed is as instructive as *that* he prayed:

> O LORD God of heaven, the great and awesome God who keeps covenant and steadfast love with those who love him and keep his commandments, let your ear be attentive and your eyes open, to hear the prayer of your servant that I now pray before you day and night for the people of Israel your servants, confessing the sins of the people of Israel, which we have sinned against you. Even I and my father's house have sinned. We have acted very corruptly against you and have not kept the commandments, the statutes, and the rules that you commanded your servant Moses. Remember the word that you commanded your servant Moses, saying, "If you are unfaithful, I will scatter you among the peoples, but if you return to me and keep my commandments and do them, though your outcasts are in the uttermost parts of heaven, from there I will gather them and bring them to the place that I have chosen, to make my name dwell there." They are your servants and your people, whom you have redeemed by your great power and by your strong hand. O Lord, let your ear be attentive to the prayer of your servant, and to the prayer of your servants who delight to fear your name, and give success to your servant today, and grant him mercy in the sight of this man (Nehemiah 1:5-11).

Note how Nehemiah personally shared in the responsibility for Israel. He willingly embraced the guilt of his nation, though his brief footnote after the prayer ("Now I was cupbearer to the king") indicates he may have held no direct guilt for their disgrace. Sin is personal, but never private. God's people corporately share in both God's blessings and the Church's failings. And so, we (Sean and John) speak in this chapter as much to ourselves as we do to our brothers and sisters in Christ. We are very aware of our own failings as Christians, as friends, as dads and as men. It's risky to speak about repentance, but we cry out for God's grace and compassion for ourselves and for others wounded by sin.

Cultural reform and church renewal are closely connected. William Wilberforce's anti-slavery movement would not have succeeded without the momentum from the Wesleyan revivals. John Wesley was a staunch opponent of slavery and saw Wilberforce's work as an expression of God's work in the Church and the world. In one of his last letters to Wilberforce, Wesley wrote:

> Unless the divine power has raised you up to be as "Athanasius against the world," I see not how you can go through your glorious enterprise in opposing that execrable villainy, which is the scandal of religion, of England, and of human nature. Unless God has raised you up for this very thing, you will be worn out by the opposition of God and devils. But if God be for you, who can be against you? Are all of them stronger than God? O, be not weary of well doing![7]

In their book *A God-Sized Vision: Revival Stories that Stretch and Stir*, Collin Hansen and John Woodbridge describe characteristics common to Church renewal: prayer, repentance, the gospel, humility and boldness.[8] It's worth asking whether these traits are present in our own lives and churches, and whether God is using increasing cultural pressure to call us back to Him. If He is, we should follow Nehemiah's lead and pray—not once and not twice, but continually. Repentance is the next step.

God's Gracious Gift of Repentance

The Bible describes repentance as one of God's best gifts, to be embraced with gratitude, not resisted out of fear or shame. It is proof, Paul wrote to the church in Rome, of God's *kindness*.[9] By leading us to see our failures, God graciously leads us to restored lives. The call to repentance is a unique privilege that God's people should welcome. Through it, God provides three things we can never achieve on our own.

First, through repentance we are made right with God. It's beautiful that the God we offend enables us to be reconciled to Him. When we are, it exemplifies to the world that God is real and present and has not abandoned the broken cultures or broken lives committed to denying Him.

Second, repentance reconciles broken relationships. This is more than "I said I was sorry, so you must forgive me." Those who otherwise would be enemies actually can be reconciled to one another. This pleases God.

Reconciliation is desperately needed between Christians and LGBT communities. People are never our real enemies. Might it be possible to maintain our convictions about homosexual behavior and same-sex unions while building bridges instead of walls? Chick-fil-A president Dan Cathy proved it is. After his comments about gay marriage on a radio program created a national uproar, Cathy personally reached out to Shane Windemeyer, the man who had organized a national campaign against him and his restaurant chain. Windemeyer revealed their surprising friendship (as well as his decision to suspend the national campaign against Chick-fil-A) after he attended the Chick-fil-A Bowl Game as a personal guest of the Cathy family:

> Throughout the conversations Dan expressed a sincere interest in my life, wanting to get to know me on a personal level. He wanted to know about where I grew up, my faith, my family, even my husband, Tommy. In return, I learned about his wife and kids and gained an appreciation for his devout belief in Jesus Christ and his commitment to being "a follower of Christ" more than a "Christian." Dan expressed regret and genuine sadness when he heard of people being treated unkindly in the name of Chick-fil-A—but he offered no apologies for his genuine beliefs about marriage.[10]

This sort of bridge building requires humility. There is too great of a difference in the morality that is being demanded by the Church and the morality that is seen in the Church. There are discrepancies in the love and forgiveness we proclaim and the love and forgiveness we portray. At least, we must admit, that is the public perception.

We are not saying our reputation is completely accurate, and we find it odd when the *New York Times, Huffington Post* or *Time* arrogantly pontificate about what they think Christianity should become. It's sometimes humorous, often offensive, and always irritating to be told what to believe from those who don't know the difference between a crosier and a "crow's ear."[11]

At the same time, whenever Christians fail to live up to what we know to be true, we are called to repent and, whenever appropriate, acknowledge our wrongdoing to those we have offended, even if they are on "the other side" of an issue. Same-sex marriage has become so contentious that the arguments for and against it are not even being heard anymore. Say you are for it, and it matters not whether you have a good reason for it. Say you are against it, and your words are dismissed no matter how articulate and thoughtful. Repentance is the only possible way past the "us vs. them" logjam in the current debate.

Third, repentance strengthens our own moral convictions. We are much more likely to cave in to wrong thinking and wrongdoing when we sweep our failures under the rug. Repentance not only restores us to God and repairs our relationships with others, but also in a very real sense, it is the only way to be our true selves. Through repentance, we become more like the people God calls us to be. This, in turn, models to those in the LGBT community that true identity is only found in Christ not in sexuality.

The biblical word for all that repentance accomplishes is "reconciliation" (2 Corinthians 5:18-19). Reconciliation implies that broken relationships are repaired, restored and renewed. When we are reconciled to God in Christ, Paul says (twice) that we become reconcilers. In light of these incredible promises, *why wouldn't we repent?*

Maybe we don't know how. Repentance is, for some Christians, a word oft-repeated and rarely practiced. The following prayer has guided God's people for many generations:

Most merciful God,
We confess that we have sinned against you in thought, word, and deed, by what we have done, and by what we have left undone. We have not loved you with our whole heart; we have not loved our neighbors as ourselves.

We are truly sorry and we humbly repent. For the sake of your Son Jesus Christ, have mercy on us and forgive us; that we may delight in your will, and walk in your ways, to the glory of your Name.

Amen.[12]

Whether we choose these words or not, they clarify the scope of our guilt before God and others. We are guilty for things both done and left undone. We are guilty for not loving God properly and not loving our neighbors properly. And we seek restoration to God's will, not just an alleviation of guilt.

So, we must ask ourselves difficult questions about our attitudes and actions:

- Have we told inappropriate jokes that dehumanize gays and lesbians?
- Have we treated some persons differently because of what we knew or suspected about their sexual orientation?
- Have we listened as someone entrusted us with his or her deep struggles with sexual identity or behaviors, only to break off the relationship in disgust or fear?
- Have we slandered others, whether or not they've slandered us first?
- Have we spread gossip?
- Have we condemned another, using their homosexual sin to justify and coddle our own heterosexual sin?
- Have we re-tweeted or re-posted harsh and uncharitable words about the gay community on Facebook?
- Have we physically or emotionally abused someone because they identify as gay?

If you can answer no to all of these questions, we hope you won't think yourself to be better than others. Remember, we share in the wins and losses of the Christian community. My (Sean's) heart broke recently when a gay atheist told my students that Christians have been his greatest enemy. How sad that he doesn't know Christians as those who extend love, grace and understanding, even if we see the issue itself differently.

And remember, it's not only what we have done; it's also what we have left undone. Have we allowed a disagreement about same-sex marriage to end a relationship without doing everything we could? Have we failed to defend the truth about marriage when we knew we should have? Have we been intimidated into silence when we should have spoken up? Have we failed to stand up for someone being mocked and dehumanized because of his or her sexual orientation? Has our interaction with those in the gay community, as well as those who promote same-sex marriage, been marked by compassion?

That last question, we think, is critical. If we will speak and act with gentleness and compassion, we will win over more people. Many will see our convictions as convictions, rather than as bullying self-righteousness. We won't win over everyone, of course, but we will win over more people than we have.

But more than that, compassion is what God expects of us. Peter told a group of Christians being persecuted and dispersed that their defense of the gospel should be done with "gentleness and respect" (1 Peter 3:15). It wasn't a suggestion. It was a command.

How we treat others reflects what we really believe about the gospel. In Matthew 18, Jesus told a parable about a servant who owed his master a debt so great that he could not repay it. He appealed to his master for more time, and his master graciously forgave him the entire debt. But the same servant failed to forgive another for a much smaller debt. When his master found out, he was furious! "Should not you have had mercy on your fellow servant," the master demanded, "as I had mercy on you?" (Matthew 18:33).

If we are truly aware of how much we have been forgiven, we will have more compassion for gay people. As long as we think we are better, or overlook our own sins of gossip, lust, sloth or envy, we will be unable to truly love gay people (and really *all* people) with the love Jesus wants us to demonstrate. Recognizing the depth of our own sin will help us be more gracious with others.

The Good News

Repentance ends with good news, not bad. We are forgiven! Admitting our own failures first should not lead us to silence and shame. Rather, it enables us to speak and act in truth and love.

So, Christian, know the assurances of God's forgiveness. From the apostle Paul to his protégé Timothy: "The saying is trustworthy and deserving of full acceptance, that Christ Jesus came into the world to save sinners, of whom I am the foremost" (1 Timothy 1:15). From the apostle John in his first epistle: "If we confess our sins, he is faithful and just to forgive us our sins and to cleanse us from all unrighteousness" (1 John 1:9); and in the next chapter, "if anyone does sin, we have an advocate with the Father, Jesus Christ the righteous. He is the propitiation for our sins, and not for ours only but also for the sins of the whole world" (1 John 2:1-2). And from our savior Jesus Christ: "Come to me, all who labor and are heavy laden, and I will give you rest. Take my yoke upon you, and learn from me, for I am gentle and lowly in heart, and you will find rest for your souls" (Matthew 11:28-29).

The gospel is not just for the lost. It's for us too. We need to hear it over and over, especially as we seek to stand for truth and to love people. Repentance brings humility, and humility fosters boldness. We'll need plenty of both for the days ahead.

The Church's Response to Same-Sex Marriage

AN INTERVIEW WITH MATTHEW LEE ANDERSON

Why does it seem the Church is so quickly culturally marginalized on issues relating to sex and marriage?

We have often failed to understand the deep roots of our Christian position on sex and marriage. As a result, we end up speaking about same-sex marriage in ways that do not draw people toward the good news. The necessary no to same-sex acts that the Christian witness demands must be enfolded and structured by the yes that God gives to people in Jesus Christ.

Of course, it is possible that people will still reject us once they hear the no, but that is not our responsibility—it is our task to describe the shape of reality with respect to human sexuality, which includes announcing to the world the forgiveness that Christ has offered on the cross to all of us for our sins and transgressions.

As you look at everyday Christians in the West today, where are the holes in our theology when it comes to sex and marriage that have enabled same-sex marriage to make such headway into our culture?

The absence of a deep and fundamental commitment to *chastity* as guiding every part of our lives is among the most pervasive problems with the Church today. Ironically, it is the pure of heart who are able to see all things—which means that if we are not chaste ourselves, then we will fail to see the ways in which our lives are entangled within the same worldliness and fallenness that are at the heart of the case for same-sex marriage.

Additionally, though it may seem counterintuitive, Christians in the West often have a deeply problematic understanding of children and their role within the marriage and the family. In our resistance to a culture where children have been marginalized and rejected, many Christians have idolized them and sacrificed their whole lives for them. Without a living commitment to children as *gifts* from God, though, the intuitions that stand beneath the gay marriage case become much more plausible.

What are the biggest mistakes Christians have made so far in dealing with homosexuality and same-sex marriage?

Christians have tended to be reactionary and defensive in dealing with homosexuality and same-sex marriage. The moment we become defensive of marriage in our culture is the moment that we misunderstand it. Biblical marriage must be advanced, first in our own hearts and minds through nurture and care and then in our communities and in our broader society.

Because the Christian position on homosexuality and marriage was accepted for so long, I think many Christians assumed that the disputes would be easy. We haven't done the philosophical or argumentative exploration necessary to try to explain the foundational principles of this issue to people, in part because we haven't had to for . . . oh, at least 2,000 years.

Christians also haven't been people marked by joy. Yes, the message of Christ can be tough and unpopular, but Jesus is Lord and all will be well. Eat, drink, be merry and make the arguments—because tomorrow is in the hands of God.

Matthew Lee Anderson is the lead writer at Mere Orthodoxy.com and author of *Earthen Vessels: Why Our Bodies Matter to God* and *The End of Our Exploring: A Book About Questioning and the Confidence of Faith.*

AN INTERVIEW WITH S. MICHAEL CRAVEN

Is it time for the Church to divorce the State?

By every objective account, the Church in America today finds itself immersed in a culture that is decisively post-Christian, meaning the structures of Christendom have been supplanted by secular leaders and ideologies that now guide our culture-forming institutions. No amount of reluctance to accept this fact will change the situation; therefore the Church, as it has throughout history, must reconsider its missiology and tactics if it hopes to offer an effective and faithful witness.

With the coming of Christ, Christians began to proclaim and display a new understanding of marriage on many levels, but more uniquely as a sacramental union that had its foundations in the relationship between Christ and His church. It wasn't until the fourth century that clerics began to function as civil authorities relative to marriage when the settlement of joining the church to the Roman Empire was becoming firm. Once bishops and priests became civil authorities, the civil and religious dimensions of marriage also became inextricably joined—a situation that has endured to this day.

In those states where SSM has been codified into law, I'm afraid the time has come for the Church to sever its alliance with a state that presumes to reorder what God has ordered. This is not an abandonment of marriage, merely a declaration that the Church of Jesus Christ will no longer function as a civil magistrate on behalf of a government that declares the fundamental Christian understanding of marriage and the natural family to be void. The Church would, of course, continue to perform Christian marriage ceremonies symbolizing the sacred union of a man and a woman, but only for its covenant members. To satisfy the legal dimensions of marriage, Christian couples would obtain marriage licenses and the like from civil authorities—one ceremony sacramental and the other civil.

There would, in essence, follow two classes of marriage with two different understandings of obligations and values: Christian and civil. The world would be at liberty to pursue its version of "marriage" and all of the associated consequences while the Church would remain at liberty to do likewise. If marriage and the natural family are to be ordered as God describes, then we can predict with certainty that Christian marriages and families will more often thrive, while those marriages constructed under a disordered view will more often flounder. This, of course, assumes that "Christian" marriages are in fact *Christian* in their understanding and practice—an assumption that may be generous to say the least and an area to which the Church might want to devote more attention before attacking the world's perverse view of marriage.

While I do not wish to see families of any persuasion fail to flourish given the personal and social devastation that follows, the Church has spoken life to a stiff-necked and unbelieving culture—yet they have chosen the road that leads to death. Thus, the only remedy may be the realization of those inevitable consequences, which by God's grace I pray bring repentance.

While many may perceive this as grounds for pessimism, Church history demonstrates that the faithfulness of the Church is often most vital when the contrast between the kingdoms of God and this world are the most severe. The call upon the faithful in our time may be one in which we first re-evangelize the *Church* with the full-orbed "gospel of the Kingdom." Clearly, the escapist evangelicalism of the twentieth century lacks the theological and spiritual substance necessary to challenge a depraved culture. Since judgment begins in the house of the Lord, perhaps we should seek to recover our own faith and witness by warning the Church and teaching the Church with all wisdom, that we may present everyone mature in Christ (see Colossians 1:28), rather than being overly concerned with political strategies aimed at stopping fallen men from doing what fallen man is, by nature, inclined to do.

Let us instead bear witness to the in-breaking rule and reign of God (i.e., the Kingdom), being obedient in loving God and loving others, by being the righteous people of God who intentionally *disadvantage themselves* for the sake of others!

S. Michael Craven is the founder of Battle for Truth and the author of *Uncompromised Faith: Overcoming Our Culturalized Christianity*. Michael also serves as the chairman and CEO of The Good-Works Company, "an uncommon company for the common good," that works to alleviate poverty and promote human flourishing through the provision of meaningful employment to the poor.

The Church and Same-Sex Marriage: A To-Do List

"It's over," he told me (John) grimly. *"We've lost."*

These words came from a wounded warrior, a pastor who had dedicated much of his ministry to calling Christians to apply their faith in the public square and to opposing things like same-sex marriage. But his side, which he had spent so much time and energy defending, had been, he thought, definitively defeated. He was licking his wounds and wondering what to do next.

Sentiments like these are not unusual, and we can sympathize with them. But we also hope they don't last too long. The legal status of something alters neither its truthfulness nor its claim on our lives. As Christians, we are still responsible to the institution of marriage as God intended it, just as we are still responsible for unborn children, regardless of whether abortion is legal.

The pro-life movement was launched from the devastating loss of *Roe v. Wade,* an unexpected and intrusive Supreme Court decision that established a nationwide legal right to abortion on demand and without restrictions.[1] Many thought that with the *Roe* decision, the abortion debate was effectively over. But it was not. Instead, a small, often disconnected but committed group of people championed the dignity of every human life in spite of what the Supreme Court said.[2] Thirty years later, public opinion has shifted away from abortion without restrictions; state-level regulations have put many abortion providers out of business; and the 2014 abortion rate reached its lowest point since 1973.[3] "Forty years ago abortion-rights activists won an epic victory with *Roe v. Wade*," said a January 2013 cover of *Time* magazine. "They've been losing ever since."[4]

Those of us hoping to build a strong marriage culture can learn from the pro-life movement. Like us, they faced an uphill cultural battle. They too were accused of being "on the wrong side of history," destined to die out in a generation or two. And yet, they've made great strides. We can learn a thing or two. Or three.

The first lesson is that cultural activism is always more effective when accompanied by personal care. "What about the women who resorted to back alley abortions because they had nowhere to turn?" abortion advocates have cried for years. And "What about all the unwanted children? Who's going to care for them?" In response, pro-life women, mostly Christians, opened care centers in just about every community in America. Women facing unplanned pregnancies were given counseling, support, child-rearing classes, free ultrasounds, adoption information, diapers and car seats. More recently, Christian couples began adopting in record numbers. Though, in reality, back-alley abortion statistics were ridiculously inflated,[5] and well-meaning activists and adoptive parents weren't always perfect, a powerful argument for abortion was contradicted.

The second lesson is that there are always ways to get the full story out, even when it is being suppressed. So many people today have seen close-up views of unborn life provided by advanced ultrasound technology and improved prenatal care that the "it's just a clump of cells" talking point for abortion just isn't as convincing anymore.[6] Pro-lifers learned that images, including properly used graphic images, expose the horrendous reality of abortion.[7] When not hidden behind sterilized nomenclature, abortion is difficult to defend.

Currently the stories most often told about same-sex marriage are ones of personal fulfillment and courageous acts of "coming out" and "being true to oneself." But there are also stories of abandoned and broken families, courageous chastity, and redeemed lives. When heterosexual adultery breaks up a marriage, everyone calls it wrong. When it is a gay affair, suddenly it's a cause to celebrate. This is the story of Janna, a lady I (John) met in Seattle. Her husband left their marriage to pursue a gay lover, but she doesn't think it was "for the best." She'll tell you she was abandoned and her children were hurt by her former husband's quest for fulfillment. Janna's story deserves to be heard too.

The third lesson that can be learned from the pro-life movement is that sound bites and clichés are no substitute for a clear, well-reasoned case. Over the last several decades, leading philosophers and apologists worked to clarify the moral status of the unborn, using science, theology and philosophy to support their case.[8] Then they simplified that information so that it was accessible and usable. Their hard work is now used to train an army of "pro-life apologists."[9]

Christians Can Make a Difference

Chuck Colson was right: Culture can be shifted over the backyard fence and around the barbeque grill.[10] Informed and articulate Christians can make a difference. Like those committed to defend life, those hoping to promote natural marriage must overcome reputation liabilities (deserved and undeserved), a firmly entrenched counter mindset, and the difficulty of presenting a winsome and reasonable case for our position. The pro-life movement has succeeded in bringing clarity to an issue draped in noise and confusion. Promoters of natural marriage can too.[11]

We should be encouraged to know that it can happen, and we have no excuse for not doing everything we can. Marriage is just too important. In light of these lessons gleaned from our pro-life forbears, here are a few ideas:

1. We can change our reputation from those who hate gays to those who love them.

Christians have been guilty of demonizing those with same-sex attraction or gender identity struggles and those engaged in homosexual behavior. In *After the Ball*, Kirk and Madsen described numerous incidents where individuals who identify as gay, lesbian or transgender have suffered unjustly. Few Christians, of course, would ever think of doing such evil to someone else, but anytime it happens, it is wrong.

Not all of the trumpeted stories of abuse and discrimination are true. In recent years, tales of waiters receiving anti-gay script on restaurant receipts instead of tips,[12] parents refusing invitations on behalf of their children to birthday parties,[13] and hate speech spray painted on garage doors[14] almost all have been proven false. Even the most notorious tale of gay hate is not the story it's been made out to be, it seems. After years of investigating the murder of Matthew

Shepard, award-winning journalist Stephen Jiminez concluded that the murder was most likely the result of a drug-induced rage, not homophobic hate.[15]

Even an infinite number of fabrications, however, can never justify a single mistreatment. On a purely pragmatic level, mistreatment has motivated certain gay activists to eliminate any and all dissent on homosexual behavior and gay marriage. As Ross Douthat wrote, "Christians had plenty of opportunities—thousands of years' worth—to treat gay people with real charity, and far too often chose intolerance. (And still do, in many instances and places.) So being marginalized, being sued, losing tax-exempt status—this will be uncomfortable, but we should keep perspective and remember our sins, and nobody should call it persecution."[16]

But far more important than cultural comfort is the reputation of Christ. Whenever we fail to treat anyone with the dignity they deserve as created image-bearers of God, we compromise our Christian witness. That simply should never be.

We must, of course, speak our convictions about marriage and sexual fidelity whenever necessary, and we know that even when we speak in love and grace, we risk cultural ire. But the truth is, "The church's anti-homosexual reputation isn't just a reputation for opposing gay sex or gay marriage; it's a reputation for hostility to gay people."[17] We can argue about whether the reputation is deserved or not, but our energy would be better spent working to change it.

It starts with the next person we meet. The reality is that far too often, our claims to love those struggling with sexual identity issues or those trapped in homosexual sin sound hollow if not evidenced by actions. Love is not passive.

Some years ago I (Sean) attended the summer Olympics with my family in Atlanta. My sister and I were working for a T-shirt stand inside Centennial Park when a man wearing a shirt covered with a large rainbow flag approached our booth. I asked him which country the flag represented. "Oh, it's just a queer thing," he responded. "You see, I'm gay." In a matter-of-fact manner I asked him if people made fun of him for being gay. He responded immediately, "Oh yeah, I get demeaning statements thrown at me all the time."

I looked right at him. I could see a man who had been hurt and broken by the taunts and ridicule of others. I felt compassion for him and disgust at how people had treated him. So I told him, "I'm really sorry that people have treated you that way. It's not right."

He thanked me over and over again. "You're the nicest person I have met at the entire Olympics," he said, and then asked if he could get a picture of us together. I have never seen him since, and we didn't talk about the gospel. I simply tried to treat him as a human being made in the image of God, as I believe God wants us to treat *everyone*. I wish I could say that I've always treated people this way, but that wouldn't be true. All human beings deserve respect regardless of race, gender, age, socioeconomic status, sexual orientation, or any other status that is secondary to being an image-bearer of God.

God loves all people, and so should we. The message of Jesus is the same to all sinners, including us: "I am the resurrection and the life. Whoever believes in me, though he die, yet shall he live, and everyone who lives and believes in me shall never die. Do you believe this?" (John 11:25-26).

2. We must tell the truth about same-sex attraction, homosexual sin and same-sex marriage.

It's tempting to downplay biblical morality to make Christianity more palatable. But loving others requires that we tell the truth, including, when necessary, that homosexual behavior is a sin. It isn't loving to mislead people and suggest that God approves of any and all sexual behavior. He doesn't.

Note that we did not say that homosexual inclinations are necessarily a sin. Unfortunately, some Christians, often out of deep concern for those struggling with same-sex attraction, promise that Christ will change one's orientation from gay to straight. He might. Many, like Rosario Butterfield, have experienced a change in their sexual orientation.[18] Others, like Wesley Hill, did not.[19] We should neither make false promises about change in orientation nor ignore its possibility. We must tell the truth.

On the other hand, too many Christians conclude that God must be okay with homosexual behaviors or else He would take those inclinations away.[20] This denies the historic, consistent witness of the Church to the testimony of the Scripture. Any sexual activity outside the given norms of marriage is sin. We must tell the truth.

Christ promised to save us from sin and empower us to overcome temptation, but He never promised to remove our inclinations. Single Christians face the consistent struggle of opposite-sex attraction. The temptations will remain, but perpetual attractions or inclinations do not remove our responsibility to obedience. We must tell the truth.

One elephant in the room is whether homosexuality is a choice. Many Christians insensitively repeat over and over that it is, but to many of the men and women we have talked with who struggle with same-sex attraction, it isn't. They look at their lives and say, "I would have never chosen this. I can't choose *not* to feel this way. I've tried to feel straight, but nothing has changed." We believe them.

We must be careful with our words. When we say homosexuality is a choice, are we referring to inclinations or behaviors? The best information available on the roots of same-sex attraction suggests that it is often a mix of nature and nurture. While factors such as abuse and strained family relationships *may* contribute to the direction of sexual attractions for some, it's not true of everyone. For example, theologian and author Wes Hill does not trace his same-sex attraction to past hurts or relational problems, but to the theological reality that human nature is fallen. Still, Hill says, he is responsible to be chaste in obedience to God's design.[21] Like Hill, we must tell the truth.

3. We can stop implying in our words and actions that homosexual sin is worse than all other sexual sins, and that sexual sins are unforgiveable.

We live in an age of culture-wide sexual brokenness. As G. K. Chesterton once said, "There are many ways to fall down, but there's only one way to stand up straight." Too often, homosexuality is singled out as "what's wrong with America" while other sexual sins get a wink and a nod. This is wrong.

We aren't saying that all sins are equal. Some sins are worse than others, in consequence and in offense to God, contrary to the oft-repeated cliché (see Proverbs 6:16-19; Matthew 23:23; John 19:11). But in the biblical lists of those sins that God especially hates, sexual immorality of all types is identified, along with rebellion, lying and idolatry.[22] The reality is that none of us is "better off" than anyone else in terms of our guilt before God. That's why it's so misguided and insidious to act as if we somehow are more deserving of grace because we don't struggle with *that* sin. We aren't any more deserving than anyone else.

There is a unity in God's law, which is portrayed in James 2:10: "For whoever keeps the whole law but fails in one point has become accountable for all of it." Though not all sins are equal, all of us stand equally as sinners and lawbreakers before God. With this in mind, we should have more grace towards those whose struggle is different than our own.

A specific application of this truth for the Church is that same-sex attraction does not disqualify someone from Christian faith or service any more than other temptations do. If someone is living in obedience to God's will, we should welcome their presence and, if appropriate, their leadership. Like all members of the body, we need them as much as they need us (see 1 Corinthians 12:14-26). In an age of such extensive sexual compromise in the Church, perhaps God is raising up men and women who are overcoming this temptation to help His people.

4. We can defend the religious liberty of all Americans.

In several high-profile disputes, gay or lesbian couples have accused private business owners of discrimination in cases that will shape our nation's future on religious liberty. District judges in Colorado, New Mexico and elsewhere have declared that business owners may not refuse their services for same-sex union ceremonies, even if it violates their deeply held convictions.

There are two questions in each of these scenarios. First, to what extent should a Christian participate in a same-sex wedding ceremony? Christians can have a legitimate debate about that. Second, should the government force someone to participate in a ceremony if it violates his or her conscience? That's a different question, indeed. Conscience rights are precious and worth protecting.

To guard their own religious freedom, Christian business owners should be able to demonstrate (and document) a clear track record of how faith shapes day-to-day operations. They must draw clear ethical lines, and they must be consistent in holding those lines, especially when it comes to sexuality and marriage. For example, I (John) have a friend who runs a bakery. Because of his Christian convictions, he turns down any requests for genitalia-shaped cakes. If he is asked to bake a cake for a same-sex wedding, he can demonstrate he's been consistent in other areas. Though he may still face consequences for his decision, his decision has been made ahead of time and his policies are documented. This strengthens his legal claim to First Amendment conscience rights.

It is vital that all of us defend religious freedom. Even if it is not our heads on the proverbial chopping block, it may be soon enough. No Christian should sit this one out.

Christians must distinguish between discriminating against a gay person and refusing to participate in certain behaviors. Christian should never refuse services to someone because they identify as gay or lesbian. Our actions are to be based on convictions, not hate.

5. We can tell better stories about love, sex, marriage and family.

The current crop of cultural storytellers is telling this story as they see it, and it isn't helping our cause. We need pro-marriage artists to engage people at the level of their imagination. We need to hear and see stories that reflect the beauty of life-long married love in a compelling way. People must *see* the good of marriage in action.

One of our favorite television shows is *Shark Tank*, where hopeful entrepreneurs pitch their businesses to high-powered venture capitalists. Even during times of economic downturns, this show inspires people to believe in the power of hard work and innovation. A seminar presentation arguing for personal responsibility and the good of business is not nearly as effective as *Shark Tank* has been by embodying these truths.

Couldn't we do the same with marriage? Couldn't churches highlight couples in the congregation who have stuck together for years? Couldn't artists make movies and write songs with stories that will inspire people to believe, once again, in marriage? Couldn't graphic designers create compelling Internet memes that can be forwarded and shared? Simply put, we need some sort of answer to the simple and persuasive "marriage equality" tagline that dominates Facebook.[23]

Simplistic "happily ever after" stories won't do. White-washed portrayals of family life where the house is always clean, the money always there, the sex always great, and the children always bathed and attentive at devotions will only disappoint in the long run. Christians often tell utopian stories about marriage and family, in which all conflicts are neatly fixed by an apology and prayer. Life is more complex and broken than those stories acknowledge, but the gospel is big enough for the worst that reality has to offer. Our stories, songs, movies and books should be too.

We need to tell stories of marriages that last. As we write this chapter, my (John's) grandmother is walking her husband of 72 years through the final difficult months of his life. While painful to watch, my entire family and their community are seeing the raw beauty of life-long married love.

We also need to tell (and see) stories of marriages that overcame infidelity, life-changing disability, or great loss. We need to see and to know that forgiveness, faithfulness and redemption are possible. This will help people believe in marriage again.

6. We need to expect the conversations about marriage and be ready for them when they come.

It's maddening when Christian leaders are caught off-guard when asked on national television about same-sex marriage! *The question will be asked*. The opportunity must be seized to speak the truth in love.

But we can't just offload this responsibility on Christian celebrities and spokespersons. We will be asked too, at our family dinners, in college classes and in dorm rooms, over office small talk, on airplanes and at neighborhood block parties. If not prepared when the questions arise, we will find ourselves choosing silence or compromise.

Pastor Rick Warren brilliantly demonstrated how to defend marriage while in the hot seat on *Piers Morgan Live*. When asked about same-sex marriage, he was articulate and loving, yet firm: "I fear the disapproval of God more than I fear your disapproval or the disapproval of society."[24]

Though we ought not shy away from the Christian source of our convictions, we should also know how to use prudential arguments for marriage. Marriage can be defended, as we described earlier in this book, without reference to Scripture or Christianity. For example, we can say, "Every child deserves a mom and a dad, and I cannot support any definition of marriage that leaves one of them out of a child's life." Or "Every society has recognized the need to regulate the relationship that produces and best protects children." Or:

> The equality of all persons does not equal the equality of all lifestyles or all relationships. For example, the mere fact that all persons are created equal does not mean that polygamy or incestual marriage ought therefore to be made legal. You cannot move logically from the equality of persons to the equality of actions, choices, lifestyles, or relationships. It simply does not follow.[25]

Make no mistake: Even if our words are articulate and loving, and we have a strong track record of kindness, we risk being embarrassed or ostracized. We may even face unjust consequences, like a failed grade or loss of employment. We need to be ready for that too.

 # Giving Marriage Back to the World: Suggestions for the Long Haul

I sat down to type a scathing rant about gay marriage. I sat down to tell the world that gay marriage is the greatest threat to the sanctity of marriage. But then I remembered . . . a sign I saw on the side of the road a little while back. *Divorce for sale! Only 129 dollars!*

And then I remembered an article I read last week about the new phenomenon of "divorce parties." *Divorced is the new single*, the divorce party planner tells us.

And then I remembered another article claiming that the divorce rate is climbing because the economy is recovering. *Now that things are getting a little better, we can finally splurge on that divorce we've always wanted!*

And then I remembered that . . . there is one divorce every 13 seconds, or over 46,000 divorces a week in this country. And then I remembered that . . . there are half as many divorces as there are marriages in a single year.

And then I remembered no-fault divorce. I remembered that marriage is the *ONLY LEGAL CONTRACT A PERSON CAN BREAK WITHOUT THE OTHER PARTY'S CONSENT AND WITHOUT FACING ANY LEGAL REPERCUSSIONS.*

And then I remembered how many Christian churches gave up on marriage long ago, allowing their flock to divorce and remarry and divorce and remarry and divorce and re-marry . . . And then I remembered that over 40% of America's children are growing up without a father in the home. And then I remembered that close to half of all children will witness the breakdown of their parents' marriage . . .

The institution of marriage is crumbling beneath us; it's under attack, it's mortally wounded, it's sprawled out on the pavement with bullet wounds in its back, coughing up blood and gasping for breath. And guess who did this? It wasn't Perez Hilton or Elton John, I can tell you that.[1]

The most important question is not "What are we going to do about same-sex marriage?" It is "What are we going to do about *marriage?*"

It is widely assumed that Christianity, when it rose to prominence in the Western world, stamped out all the pagan fun. By imposing its backward ideas about sex and marriage, puritanical imperialists speaking for God stole freedom and replaced it with guilt. Among those responsible for this myth was anthropologist Margaret Mead. Her book *Coming of Age in Samoa,*[2] written when she was just 23 years old, argued that sexually free Samoans were better off than their Western counterparts struggling under the burden of Christian morality. That narrative was then retrofitted on history and helped promote the increasingly popular thesis that Christianity could be blamed for almost everything that ailed the world.

Though her research has been quite thoroughly debunked (including by the Samoans she had studied[3]), the hypothesis it ultimately failed to prove remains. But it just isn't true. Christian sexual morality wasn't oppressive and Roman sexual morality wasn't free. In reality, early Christians proclaimed radical new ideas about sex in a culture of sexual violence enabled by slavery. Many men, women, boys and girls did not have the luxury of choosing to *not* participate in all of the free love going around. For them, life was abusive and dehumanizing.

In contrast, Christianity offered a view of the world that suggested that all humans, whether slave or free, were made in the image and likeness of God.[4] Though it took longer than it should have for the institution of slavery to be dismantled in the West by mostly Christian activists, the earliest Christian theologians and writers proclaimed God's call for both sexual purity and the better treatment of slaves (Philemon). As a result, new classes of people found protection, including women.

It's also widely assumed that marriage has historically been an institution that oppresses women. Certainly, many marriages earned this reputation. But overall, the sexual restraint marriage promotes provided a better cultural situation for women. Dr. Mark Regnerus explains this with what he calls the "economics of sex."[5] Think of economics as "supply and demand." The men in a society will always (well, almost always[6]) have a demand for sex, but women largely decide how much they have to pay for it. When the supply of sex is not kept low by social expectations of chastity, men can have it without having to grow up, get married or be employed. Sex is "cheap." Women give in sexually so that they can get the social goods they have a demand for, such as relational security.

In strong marriage cultures, women are able, both by social mores and stern fathers, to keep the supply of sex low. When supply is low and demand is high, the price increases. Men have to pay a price. Traditionally, that meant they had to grow up, become economically and socially stable, and gain a father's permission.

Of course, no culture is perfect, and wrongly understood and practiced, marriage can be a prison. Rightly understood and practiced, however, it brings protection and freedom. A culture where sexuality is not tied to marriage is one in which the most vulnerable, especially women and children, are without one of their most effective protections.[7] We need look no further than the contemporary "hook-up" culture that, when combined with the Internet pornography free-for-all, hyper-sexualizes both women and children.

Even feminists and left-leaning politicians are realizing this. In 2013, the Interior Minister of Iceland proposed a nationwide ban of online pornography in order, she said, to protect their children.[8] Shortly after, the European Parliament voted on a ban of all forms of pornography,[9] and British Prime Minister David Cameron proposed legislation that would change the default setting on Internet filters to block pornography unless a user specifically requested it, after several high-profile sexually related crimes in Great Britain.[10]

Do you see what this means? A culture in which sex is cheap is a culture in which people are devalued. Consider, for example, the worldwide scourge of sex trafficking. But it's also notable that the fight to end sex trafficking is the most popular cause *du jour*, one currently championed by Christians and non-Christians alike.

This is among the many signs that people are growing weary of the brutal consequences of so-called sexual "freedom."

What Christians Have to Offer the World

For many, there is no real way out of this cheap-sex culture. Christians, if we are aware, will find redemptive opportunities all around us. We can propose the good gifts of marriage and sexual wholeness to a culture whose sexual ethic is bringing slavery instead of freedom. As we do so, we can point people to Jesus Christ, the ultimate source of all freedom. The converse is also true. Broken people know they need help. We could see an incredible openness to the gospel in the days ahead as people reach the end of their self-imposed slavery. In Christ, they can find a better way.

Christian, have hope. We still have much to offer the world.

1. We can teach and model what marriage is and how it fits in God's plan.

A recent Pew Research study found that an increasing number of Americans considers marriage to be *obsolete*.[11] It's one thing to think marriage is good or bad, but it's quite another to think it just doesn't matter. Beyond getting marriage *wrong*, the evidence shows that as a culture we just don't *get marriage*. Something akin to the biblical vision for marriage was the default cultural setting for generations. How did it lose its cultural place?

For all the seminars and sermons offered by churches across America teaching how to have a "happy" marriage, a "fulfilled" marriage or a "meaningful" marriage, there are precious few that disciple believers about God's intent and design for marriage.[12] For many Christians, their faith is moral decoration on a view of marriage they inherited from culture. All the seminars and the sermons in the world that approach marriage pragmatically, but fail to unseat the idea that marriage exists to honor our feelings and further our happiness, will only succeed in reinforcing and perpetuating the thinking that undermines marriage.

The critical fight is for definitions. The battle of ideas is quite often the battle over the definition of words. For example, there is incredible confusion about the meaning of love.

Several years ago, I (John) incurred the wrath of a group of girls when I mocked the movie *The Notebook* in their school chapel. After my talk, I was quickly cornered by three of them (including a teacher) who angrily asked, "How could you not like a movie with such a great picture of love?"

They were referring to how the older man in the film was faithful to visit his bride day after day, even when she was unable to remember him. Every day at her nursing facility, the man would retell their love story to her. She would remember who he was because of the story, and they would share a few warm moments together before dementia stole her mind away again. "The man's behavior is a great picture of love," I admitted to my questioners. "But the problem is the story. It cannot produce that ending!"

The Notebook's story line is typical: two teenagers are possessed by the passionate, strong feelings they have for each other. These feelings never go away, despite the hard times they face, the commitments they break, the selfishness they display, and the poor character they exhibit. What definition of love does that assume?

Love in *The Notebook* is nothing more than strong feelings. But feelings are fickle and cannot sustain the lifelong faithful commitment the movie claimed it could. In the movie, feelings last forever. In real life, forever love requires commitment, effort, forgiveness and sacrifice.

Do you see how this wrong thinking impacts marriage? If love is something we fall into, it's also something we fall out of. If love is nothing more than strong emotions, the commitments stop when the emotions stop. And, as we see far too often, so too ends the marriage. At weddings, couples vow to "love each other as long we both shall live." But unless they base those vows on something more than emotions, the reality will be that they'll only "live together as long as we both shall love."

"Freedom" is another word requiring careful definition. If freedom is nothing more than a "free for all," then any rules restricting our freedom are out the window. We live that way today, and we have all the accompanying addictions to prove it. That definition of freedom only enslaves us to our passions.

What if, instead, freedom is connected to responsibility, purpose and design? What if freedom is not the right to do whatever we want, but the ability to do and be what we *ought*? Unfettered freedom is destructive. Marriage brings incredible freedom, but only when properly understood.

It won't do to just shout our definitions from the pulpits and lecterns of the Church. We must carefully argue (in the best sense of the word) for them, reasoning with people about why what we believe is actually true. Take it from this Millennial letter writer, whose self-professed "change of heart" on same-sex marriage led, in part, to her decision to abandon the Christian faith altogether:

> You see SSM [same sex marriage] advocates as employing emotive arguments in order to win, but you have to realize that a lot of the Christians that are being argued against have traded in nothing but emotion for the last 30 years. . . In all the years I was a member, my evangelical church made exactly one argument about SSM. It's the argument I like to call the Argument from Ickiness: Being gay is icky, and the people who are gay are the worst kind of sinner you can be. Period, done, amen, pass the casserole. . . .
>
> The moment ickiness no longer rings true with young believers, their faith is destroyed. This is why other young ex-evangelicals I know point as their "turning point" on gay marriage to the moment they first really got to know some- one who was gay . . . In short, the anti-SSM side, and really the Christian side of the culture war in general, is responsi- ble for its own collapse. It failed to train up the young people on its own side preferring instead to harness their energy while providing them no doctrinal depth by keeping them in a bubble of emotion dependent on their never engaging with the outside world on anything but warlike terms.[13]

Those who do not understand and cannot articulate the mean- ing of marriage will either be unwilling or unable to stand against that which compromises it. The deafening silence from so many Christians about same-sex marriage indicates they don't under- stand what is at stake.

But arguments only go so far. Seeing marriage modeled is every bit as important as hearing it explained. Good marriages breed good marriages. The Church should be a place where those who want marriage mentors can find them, and where those who don't want them will get them anyway.

I (John) have taught for Summit Ministries' youth conferences since 1999. One particular summer was difficult for my wife and me.

We had just had our first child, were struggling to communicate, and were forced to live for two weeks in a somewhat nasty dorm room. I was glad when it was over.

Soon after the conference, a few of us who spoke received a letter from one of the students. "I didn't want to hear what you were teaching," she wrote, "especially about marriage. But when I watched you interact with your families, God opened my heart to what you were saying."

2. We can take a strong stand against divorce, as God does.

Because divorce is so common, condemning it risks sounding incredibly harsh to those who have personally experienced it. We do not intend to single out those who have been divorced or pretend marriage is easy or imply divorce is never justified. We both have dear friends and family members who have been through divorce. Perhaps you have experienced this form of abandonment or betrayal, or have made mistakes that resulted in a divorce. If so, our hearts and, more important, God's grace go out to you.

But we cannot ignore the clear teaching of Scripture. According to Malachi 2:13-16, divorce caused God to reject the offerings of the Israelites. It is, God says, an *act of violence* (see v. 16). According to some translations of this verse, God also says definitively, "I hate divorce."[14] Of course He does. He hates anything that so damages children, adults, communities or a nation.

We often hear that divorce rates in the Church mirror divorce rates outside of the Church. One study even suggested that the best predictor of divorce was "the concentration of conservative Protestants living in the county,"[15] but as Brad Wilcox of the University of Virginia has demonstrated, this study (and others like it) fails to distinguish between *nominal* conservative Protestants and *committed* conservative Protestants. Christians who are active in their faith, evident by religious practices like church attendance, are far less likely to get divorced than those not active in their faith.[16]

Still, this is not just about the divorce rates of individual Christians, but whether churches have committed to confront something that has caused so much hurt and destruction. Many churches have programs to help the poor, but how many intercede when a couple is contemplating divorce? Do we seek lower divorce rates as much as we seek lower school dropout rates? Do we work as hard to prepare young couples for marriage as we do to increase attendance or giving?

The church used to be the go-to place for relationships and marriage, but when a marriage is in jeopardy today, where do couples turn? Do they look to the church for help, or to professional counselors and divorce attorneys? If churches owned a proven track record for helping distressed marriages, the answer would be clear. The number of intact families in a community should become a factor by which churches measure ministry success.

Many churches do, in fact, heroically champion marriage in their communities. One large church in a major metropolitan area has set a goal of touching 10 percent of all marriages in that city, whether through pre-marital counseling, strengthening relationships, helping parents, or providing divorce intervention. The long-term impact if they succeed will be incredible since the major predictor of poverty, crime rates, graduation rates, and the overall stability of communities is marital and familial success.

On a personal level, we must have the courage to say no to divorce, both to ourselves and, when appropriate, to others. Of course, there are situations when divorce is the only option, but it's always a tragedy. And with so many in our communities impacted by divorce, we must honor our responsibility to care for its victims. How can we become surrogate families for children impacted by divorce? How can we love divorcé(e)s, embrace them into our communities, and help them heal?

3. We can honor the created connection between sex, marriage and procreation.

As difficult as it may be for many Protestants to stomach, the birth control pill was not good for the institution of marriage.[17] Somewhere in the middle of the last century, procreation was disconnected from marriage, in principle and practice. Many Christian couples today see no problem in marrying while planning to never have children, either by procreation or via adoption.[18]

But God created sex with both a *context* and with *consequences*. While the Church has been pretty clear on how sex belongs in marriage (though, alarmingly, has shown signs of compromising on this in the name of preventing abortion[19]), it has not done well in standing for the created connection between married sex and babies. This idea has spawned consequences far larger than we tend to admit.

While health, family or financial considerations *may* justify the choice to limit the number of children,[20] the most common reason is the culturally sacred idol of personal choice. Severing the tie between marriage and children compromises the role marriage plays in securing the future of a culture and furthers the destructive notion that marriage is *just* about furthering personal happiness. Plus, it obscures that one function of marriage that clearly demonstrates why marriage requires a man and a woman.

Do we teach the created connection between sex, marriage and procreation to our congregations, especially to those young couples headed for marriage? Do we help them think through the ethical implications of various methods of birth control? Do we undermine the connection between marriage and babies in some way?

When we promote chastity to teenagers, for example, by promising that "the best sex happens in marriage," and never teach the inherent relationship sex has to marriage and children, we risk reinforcing bad thinking about the purpose of sex, and therefore marriage. This amounts to Christianizing the notion that sex is only for pleasure, and marriage only for happiness. We must teach the full picture of what sex is for, not *just* that it is fun (which, of course, it is).

4. We can flee sexual immorality and seek healing for our own sexual brokenness.

Sexual sin, Paul told the church at Corinth, wrongly unites us to another person and is also a sin against oneself (see 1 Corinthians 6:9-18). One of the greatest theologians in the history of the Church, Augustine of Hippo, had a phrase for this: *homo incurvatis in se.*[21]

That's a fancy (or at least Latin) way of saying that sin leads to "humanity curved in on itself." This truth is powerfully illustrated in Oscar Wilde's novel *The Picture of Dorian Gray.*[22] Gray is a young man infatuated with his own beauty and committed to living a life of hedonism and self-fulfillment. Not wanting to age and lose his beauty, he sells his soul so that his portrait would age instead of him. Years later, his narcissism has led him to unspeakable evil, including murder. The only evidence of his guilt is the portrait that reflects his twisted soul, now horridly disfigured by his debauched choices. In an attempt to destroy the portrait that condemns him, he slashes it with a knife, but only succeeds in killing himself. The painting was undamaged.

Sin disfigures our hearts and minds. It twists us away from the people we are supposed to be. Disordered sex is particularly insidious in this way. It takes over our affections and destroys both others and us.

Nothing wreaks more havoc in our society than pornography. Dr. Mary Anne Layden, of the Sexual Trauma and Psychopathology Program of the University of Pennsylvania, told a U.S. Senate sub-committee in 2004 that pornography is every bit as addictive and destructive as compulsive gambling and heroin use. She pulled no punches in her description:

> Pornography, by its very nature, is an equal opportunity toxin. It damages the viewer, the performer, and the spouses and children of the viewers and performers. It is toxic mis-education about sex and relationships. It is more toxic the more you consume, the "harder" the variety you consume and the younger and more vulnerable the customer.[23]

Hidden evil flourishes, whether in the larger culture or in the Church. In the Church, pornography addiction has reached epidemic rates.[24] In a 2010 Witherspoon Institute study entitled *The Social Costs of Pornography,* experts from a variety of religious persuasions (atheist, Christian, Muslim, etc.) and political views agreed that pornography is destroying the fabric of our society.[25]

It is not simply destroying the wider culture; it is also deeply affecting the Church. Sean's father, Josh, considers it the greatest threat to the cause of Christ today.[26] It may be easier to pick on the issue of same-sex marriage, which is "someone else's problem," but we cannot ignore the destruction pornography is causing in our own homes and churches.

The porn epidemic may partially explain why more people are accepting same-sex marriage. In his research, Mark Regnerus found a strong correlation between heavy porn use and acceptance of same-sex relationships. We expect porn to desensitize viewers, since even so-called "straight" porn often features homoerotic activity, but Regnerus also found that men who view porn *less* are also *less* critical of the institution of marriage. The unrealistic sexual exploits depicted in pornography warp healthy expectations of marital relationships. Regnerus concludes:

> In the end, contrary to what we might wish to think, young adult men's support for redefining marriage may not be

entirely the product of ideals about expansive freedoms, rights, liberties, and a noble commitment to fairness. It may be, at least in part, a byproduct of regular exposure to diverse and graphic sex acts.[27]

At the same time, we ought never imply that sexual sin is, in any form, unforgiveable. In an age of such widespread sexual sin and brokenness, we must proclaim the full hope of the gospel. Neither heterosexual nor homosexual sin places us outside the redemptive reach of Christ.

I (John) once found myself in the awkward position of helping a young man tell his parents that his girlfriend may be pregnant. They were inconsolable. "It's all over," the mother wailed. "How could he flush his whole life down the toilet like that?" Respectfully, I stopped her. "Wait a minute," I said. "Jesus was not shocked by your son's sin, and when He went to the cross for him, this was one of the sins Christ died for." Yes, that one, and ours, and "the sins of the whole world" (1 John 2:2).

If we believe this, we must be careful with our words. Too many youth leaders and parents, in a desire to promote sexual purity, use illustrations that effectively describe sexually compromised students as used, unwanted or even disgusting. The motive is right, but the message is wrong. Christ promises to make us new, including those trapped in a homosexual lifestyle.

Unfortunately, in some Christian communities, confession of sexual struggle brings shame and shunning. We've both seen close friends treated as unclean, even after sincere repentance. More horrific is when victims of sexual abuse or assault are treated this way! What does this communicate to them and to non-believers about the grace of God? We must tell the truth about sexuality, but we are called to be healers and reconcilers (see 2 Corinthians 5:17-21) as much as we are called to be truth-tellers.

5. We need to recognize our own responsibility to the institution of marriage.

As we said in the last chapter, every Christian needs to be ready to articulately defend marriage, but there are specific roles we may be called to play. For example: *Parents*, are we modeling a biblical marriage to our children and to their friends who may not have that model in their life? Are we actively seeking to strengthen our marriages? (We recommend that parents consider attending a Weekend to Remember event, hosted by Family Life.[28]) Have we taught our kids what marriage is and why it is so important to God, as well as to a flourishing culture?

Pastor, does your congregation know that you love and cherish your wife and kids, even more than you seek the success of the next program? Have you taught the biblical view of marriage from the pulpit? Do you equip your congregation to defend natural marriage through classes, books or other resources? (A terrific resource is The Family Project study series, produced by Focus on the Family.[29]) Is your church active in the lives of married couples, offering mentoring classes as well as divorce intervention and recovery help? Is your church a safe place where people can confess sexual sin and find healing and restoration? Are you and your congregation anticipating and planning for the legal and moral challenges that are created because of same-sex marriage?

Youth workers, do you teach your students a biblical worldview of marriage? (Again, we recommend The Family Project study series by Focus on the Family.) Do you model sexual purity and a healthy marriage to your students? Do you bring older couples into your youth ministry for mentoring and modeling? Are you actively helping your students handle sexual temptation, especially pornography?

Students and singles, is there someone in your life that you look to as a model of a healthy marriage? Have you taken time to build up your understanding of marriage so that you can articulate it to others? Are you staying accountable to parents and peers about what you are looking at on the Internet? Are you skeptical about marriage? If you have been wounded by your family experience, have you sought reconciliation and forgiveness while also clarifying what is true about marriage and family? If you struggle with same-sex attraction, have you told someone? Are you actively seeking what God says about it? (And have you signed up yet for Summit? Come on, what's better than hanging out with both of us for a few days?[30])

We all have a role to play, and there's plenty we can do. If we feel defeated or demoralized by the speed and breadth in which same-sex marriage has been embraced in our society, we must start now to rebuild a culture in which the differences between it and marriage as it was created to be are obvious. In the meantime, there are specific scenarios we may face. We'll wrestle with these in the next chapter.

The Truth About Marriage and Spreading the Gospel

AN INTERVIEW WITH REVEREND TODD WAGNER

What aspects of discipleship and outreach are impacted by the cultural acceptance of same-sex marriage? In what ways should churches adjust their priorities to deal with this challenge?

Every generation has challenges that church leaders need to be aware of and prepared to equip their people to handle. Specifically, the role of those in vocational ministry is to help believers in their church bodies understand that their speech should always be filled with grace and seasoned with salt so that they should know how to respond to each person (see Colossians 4:6). First Peter 3:15 tells every believer to be ready to make a defense to everyone who asks you to give an account for the hope that is in us. If Ephesians 4:12 says that the job of a pastor is to equip the saints, not to be the Bible-answer man himself, then we are to raise up an entire community of winsome, wise, equipped Christ-followers on the matter of same-sex marriage and other issues within our culture.

Some say that standing for natural marriage gets in the way of spreading the gospel. Do you agree? Why or why not?

The gospel has legs. In other words, it suggests something. It suggests that there is a very present God who loves us and has our best interests in mind. One of the ways that churches need to engage the culture is to jump into the dialogue and offer a divine proposal—not to impose our views on others who don't see the Bible as true, but to explain why following the teachings from the Scriptures will be better for our culture. Talking about God's love of humans, expressed through the love of one man and one woman in marriage, doesn't get in the way of the gospel; it's paving the way for folks to understand God's goodness in a way that might help them receive the gospel. In fact, Paul told the church in Ephesus that marriage is one of the best illustrations of God's love that there is (see Ephesians 5:31-32).

How should churches respond when same-sex couples come to their services?

The exact same way that they do when any person living outside of the will of God comes to their services. They should love them, speak the truth to them and help them understand that God's not mad at them. Instead, He wants to set them free from things that appear life-giving and yet ultimately lead to a life that is less than best and often filled with trouble. How should churches respond to children of same-sex couples that want to be involved in the children's and youth programs? With love and grace, the same way we respond to any family that's living in a way that is contrary to God's best. We never want to punish children for choices their parents are making; rather, we should be even more compassionate, loving and specific about the goodness of God's Word and way.

Todd Wagner is the Senior Pastor and Elder at Watermark Community Church, a thriving congregation in Dallas, Texas.

So, What Now?
Guidance for
Everyday Questions

The meeting had the potential to do a great deal of harm, both to the reputation of our Christian school and to the lesbian couple that hoped to enroll their daughter. I was thankful the women had explained the situation over the phone. This gave us time to think, plan and, most important, pray.

Our school has an open enrollment policy. Families agree to support the educational philosophy and authority structure of the school, but they do not have to share our faith. Many who enrolled their children because of our academics and school culture came to love and trust Jesus Christ.

Based on our policy, I would not turn this girl away from our school, but I needed to ensure that the women knew what to expect. The day of the meeting I veered between a deep sense of disquiet and a prayerful confidence that God would enable me to speak the truth in love.

In the meeting, the women explained that someone had recommended our learning assistance program as a solution for their daughter's academic struggles. They understood we were a Christian school while admitting they were not believers.

I explained what we believed: the centrality of Jesus, forgiveness of sin, imputed righteousness, and hope for eternity. I clarified that we considered any sex outside of a heterosexual marriage to be against God's design for humanity. Then I confessed to them that the worst sinner in the room was the one speaking. As a follower of Jesus, I failed to obey Him perfectly, but my sin was done in full knowledge of His glory and love. Because of the finished work of Christ, I was trusting in Jesus alone to save me from my much-deserved fate.

I told the women that their daughter would learn the Bible, which might lead her to question their lesbian relationship. I assured them that my staff would treat them with the upmost respect, but I could not guarantee the behavior of parents in the parking lot. It couldn't be worse, they thought, than how the parents from the public school treated them.

Finally, I told them that our deepest desires, for unconditional love, lasting intimacy, significance and security, could only be satisfied by knowing and loving Jesus. And if they chose to put their daughter in our school we would point their family to Christ in every way we could. We prayed together and the meeting ended.

As they were leaving, I asked, "I know that Christians are portrayed as hateful toward you. Was I in anyway hateful or intolerant today?" With a measure of surprise they replied, "Not at all!"

I had just told a lesbian couple I had never met that they were living a sinful life and needed Jesus to rescue them, yet somehow they did not find me hateful or intolerant. They chose not to enroll their daughter, but I thanked the Lord that He allowed me to be truthful yet loving. I continue to pray they might wake to the reality of Jesus and repent and believe in Him.[1]

As same-sex marriage becomes more common, we too will face scenarios like the one above. They require a great deal of wisdom. We hope this chapter can be helpful.

But we warn you from the outset: we don't have all the answers. Sometimes, the Christian response is black or white: There are, as we've expressed throughout this book, moral absolutes about marriage, family and human sexuality. But these are uncharted cultural waters, and applying these absolutes in the context of real-life relationships and a shifting culture is tricky. It makes a difference whether one is an employer or an employee, a close family member or a stranger on an airplane, a Christian or a non-Christian.

In Romans 14, Paul instructs believers facing similar difficulties:

> One person believes he may eat anything, while the weak person eats only vegetables. Let not the one who eats despise the one who abstains, and let not the one who abstains pass judgment on the one who eats, for God has welcomed him. Who are you to pass judgment on the servant of another? It is before his own master that he stands or falls. And he will be upheld, for the Lord is able to make him stand.
>
> One person esteems one day as better than another, while another esteems all days alike. Each one should be fully convinced in his own mind.
>
> Why do you pass judgment on your brother? Or you, why do you despise your brother? For we will all stand before the judgment seat of God; for it is written, "As I live, says the Lord, every knee shall bow to me, and every tongue shall confess to God."
>
> So then each of us will give an account of himself to God. Therefore let us not pass judgment on one another any longer, but rather decide never to put a stumbling block or hindrance in the way of a brother.
>
> For the kingdom of God is not a matter of eating and drinking but of righteousness and peace and joy in the Holy Spirit. Whoever thus serves Christ is acceptable to God and approved by men. So then let us pursue what makes for peace and for mutual upbuilding (vv. 2-5,10-13,17-19).

While there are some lines that believers ought not cross (like the worship of idols, sexual immorality, gossip, etc.), there are some decisions that are matters of conscience. Similarly in 1 Corinthians, Paul says, "For why should my liberty be determined by someone else's conscience? If I partake with thankfulness, why am I denounced because of that for which I give thanks? So, whether you eat or drink, or whatever you do, do all to the glory of God" (1 Corinthians 10:29-31).

It will be difficult to wrestle through the specific situations believers will face in the days to come, so it is essential that we begin to have conversations about them now. We shouldn't wait until the heat of the moment. Pastors, leaders and parents, we need to start this conversation now and be prepared with a gracious, thoughtful response.

It matters also *how* we have the conversation. Here are a few things to keep in mind:

1. *Search the Scriptures.* We can't know God's mind on an issue without it. Though the Bible does not always provide specific guidance, it offers the framework and principles that apply to every situation.

2. *Pray for guidance, and trust God to give it.* "If any of you lacks wisdom," James instructs, "let him ask God, who gives generously to all without reproach, and it will be given him. But let him ask in faith, with no doubting, for the one who doubts is like a wave of the sea that is driven and tossed by the wind" (James 1:5-7).

3. *Don't do it alone.* "Without counsel plans fail," Proverbs 15:22 says, "but with many advisers they succeed." Communities of faith must be in this together, praying and supporting one another.

4. *Be charitable and gracious.* First, we must be gracious and hesitant to pass judgment on our Christian brothers and sisters as they walk through these difficult situations. In the age of instant social media, it is far too easy to be harsh and self-righteous without knowing all the facts. Second, we must be gracious to those on the other side of the issue, even if they make our lives miserable. As Peter wrote to a group of Christians facing increasing cultural pressure:

> But in your hearts honor Christ the Lord as holy, always being prepared to make a defense to anyone who asks you for a reason for the hope that is in you; yet do it with gentleness and respect, having a good conscience, so that, when you are slandered, those who revile your good behavior in Christ may be put to shame (1 Peter 3:15-16).

5. *Determine the lines that must not be crossed.* Daniel is a great model of this discipline. In a foreign court, he "resolved

that he would not defile himself with the king's food, or with the wine that he drank" (Daniel 1:8). He knew ahead of time where he could not compromise, and he was able to stand strong when the pressure came.

6. *Look for creative alternatives.* Patience and entrepreneurial thinking will often reveal options that at first we cannot see. For example, Daniel and his friends seemingly had only two choices: (1) violate their convictions by imbibing the king's food and drink, or (2) die. There was another alternative, however. Appealing to the head of the court, they suggested a 10-day test period in which they would eat only vegetables and trust the Lord for the results. God made them 10 times better than their peers in the court (see Daniel 1:8-20). In many cases, we may be able to find a way to keep a potential conflict from escalating, while still allowing us to follow our conscience.

7. *Avoid the victim complex.* It really doesn't help our cause if we are perceived as whiners. When it comes to our views on marriage, we will face double standards, misrepresentations and scorn. We shouldn't be surprised when it happens. Plus, Jesus promised that His followers would be hated in the world (see John 17:14).[2]

With that framework in mind, let's consider some potential scenarios.

Some What Ifs

What if a gay friend, co-worker or family member announces that they are getting married to their partner?

Everyone we meet is made in the image of God. We ought never reduce anyone to his or her sexual orientation or decision to pursue marriage. We cannot endorse a same-sex marriage, but we can treat people with dignity.

In the case of an acquaintance, distant family member or co-worker, we think it is possible to "rejoice with those who rejoice" (Romans 12:15) without rejoicing in what makes them rejoice.

In other words, we can be happy someone is happy without being happy about *why* they are happy. Responding to someone's proud announcement of his or her same-sex wedding plans with condemnation will most likely end the relationship. While saying something like, "I think that's great!" would be dishonest, we could respond by saying, "Wow! That's a huge decision. Tell me more about this person and how you met. What are you looking forward to most in marriage?" In asking these questions, we can deepen the relationship.

We may need to talk through our convictions honestly as the relationship deepens, or in the case of a close friend or family member. But the timing and environment for that conversation are critical, as well as first demonstrating that we are sincerely committed to the good of the other person.

What if I'm invited to a same-sex wedding ceremony?

We believe wedding ceremonies are sacred and that attendance implies a complicit blessing of the union itself. At a wedding, a covenant, even when not acknowledged, is being made between two people, the community and God. Therefore, we could not attend a same-sex wedding in good conscience (would we really want to "speak now or forever hold our peace" on this?).

On the other hand, a protest is rarely necessary or helpful. The extent to which Christians should verbally express disagreement will depend on how close we are to those who invite us. It may be appropriate to sit down and calmly explain our disagreement in love, but two things should already be in place. First, there should be a strong relationship. Second, as much as is possible, people should already know where we stand. It's much easier to say, "You know, I think you already know my convictions on gay relationships, so it's probably not a surprise that I cannot come to your ceremony. May we talk about this further?"

It may be that some Christians who share our convictions about marriage will choose to attend a same-sex ceremony. That is a matter of conscience. Others may choose to avoid the ceremony but join the reception and bring a gift. Others may send a gift but avoid the ceremony and reception altogether. Whatever we decide, we must act with a clear conscience before God in good faith. Realize that other Christians, in particular *young* Christians, will learn from our example.

*What if a gay friend, co-worker or family member asks me to
participate in a same-sex wedding ceremony?*

We couldn't participate in, or officiate, a same-sex wedding ceremony for the reasons given above. However, this could be a very
difficult decision for a brother asked to be the best man, or a father
asked to walk his daughter down the aisle. Even in very personal
cases like these, we would have to decline.

It's likely that if someone asks you to participate in their wedding,
you have a close relationship with them. As we said earlier, it's very
helpful to get ahead of the situation if possible. If they know where
we stand on homosexuality and same-sex marriage, yet continue to
enjoy a friendship, it may make the difficult conversation easier.

Others may come to a different decision, which brings up an
important question: How should we respond to those Christians
who choose differently about attending or participating in a same-
sex wedding ceremony? Should we break fellowship with them?

In the middle of the twentieth century, some well-meaning
conservative Christians practiced *secondary separation*. In response
to troubling trends in theology and church practice, they decided
to break fellowship not only with those who abandoned basic
Christian beliefs but also with those who held the same beliefs but
failed to break fellowship with those who abandoned them. It was
a kind of ecclesiastical "guilt by association," and it was a disaster.
It became impossible to remember who was still "clean" and who
was "unclean." In the end, these groups just isolated themselves.

Disagreement about these scenarios is inevitable, but we should
do it with grace and charity. Relationships will be strained, but
breaking fellowship should always be the last resort and only if
absolutely necessary. Remember, Jesus prayed for the unity of His
Body (see John 17:21-23).

*What if my business is asked to provide services for a
same-sex union ceremony?*

No Christian should refuse to serve a person because they are gay or
transgender. However, a distinction may be made between serving

the person and participating in their same-sex wedding. Serving a cupcake to a gay couple is not the same as baking a rainbow shaped cake with two grooms on top for their ceremony.[3] Personally, we couldn't provide services in celebration of a same-sex union. Other Christians may consider it a cost of doing business in a secular, pluralistic culture.

Though religious freedom is guaranteed in the U.S. Constitution, there is no guarantee it will hold up in front of activist judges. Still, there are ways to get ahead of the situation:

1. Describe how Christian convictions shape the company in the policy manual.
2. Document any case in which religious convictions lead to a particular job being accepted or rejected.
3. Be known as a place where everyone is welcome, and train employees specifically in relating to gay customers. If trouble arises, proof of training employees and a statement of support from a gay customer may be helpful.
4. Show genuine care for the person asking for the services. Ask questions and get a full picture of their situation before communicating the decision to them.
5. If forced to reject business, do so from the perspective of the written policy. Do not comment on the specific person soliciting the services or on their situation. Be polite and, of course, smile!
6. Refer customers to other providers who will offer the requested services. Have business cards ready.

What if I refuse and am sued for discrimination?

Contact the Alliance Defending Freedom[4] or the Beckett Fund for Religious Liberty.[5] Document everything.

*What if a same-sex couple shows up at my church and/
or wants to send their children to Sunday school?*

How would you respond if a cohabiting couple showed up at church and brought their children to Sunday school? The answer should be no different (and, hopefully, the answer is, "we would welcome them"). We can welcome people into the Church without compromising biblical standards.

When it comes to membership, leadership and receiving communion (or other ordinances considered sacred by the Church), requirements should be clearly stated in writing. Christian organizations and non-profit organizations should include convictions about human sexuality and marriage in their Statement of Faith and employment policies.

As in the story above, there's also the issue of how a larger congregation or school community will respond to the presence of same-sex couples. The time to find out is not when the first couple walks through the door. Pastors and leaders should communicate how their church or organization will treat gay and lesbian couples and their children. Appropriate training should be provided.

"But we don't want our children to see such things in church!" you may reply. Well, they will see it in culture. Why not use the Church to help Christians understand the gay lifestyle properly? This means that pastors and leaders must find ways to help parents communicate to their children age-appropriate information as it becomes necessary.

What if a gay friend, co-worker or family member begins asking me about spiritual things?

First, as you would with *anyone* asking about spiritual things, thank the Lord and ask for wisdom. Second, remember that a person is more than their sexual orientation. Everyone's deepest spiritual need is his or her need for God.

The topic may come up and, if someone accepts Christ, it should. When that time comes, we should point clearly and unapologetically to the Scriptures. First John has a lot to say about this. Do not promise more than the Scripture does, like a change in orientation. Instead, promise Christ's forgiveness and continued offer of grace to overcome temptation. And realize that this will take time. Don't expect change overnight. It's a long-term investment on your part, and theirs.

What if a person in a gay marriage becomes a Christian? Do we recommend divorce?

On one level, because same-sex marriage is not a union God (or human history) recognizes as marriage, we would suggest that a divorce in that context is not the same as a divorce in a heterosexual marriage. Ending the relationship is, in fact, a step closer for each member of the couple (even the one who disagrees) to God's design for their life.

But we shouldn't expect this too quickly. Even though a same-sex relationship is a different kind of relationship than marriage, it doesn't make a break-up any less devastating for those involved. If we lead someone to end their gay marriage, we had better be willing to walk with them through it from start to finish, with patience, love and support.

If children are involved, the situation becomes much more difficult. The church community should be there to help any child caught in the middle. The child may know the couple as his or her parents, so relationships should be preserved if at all possible. Prepare for legal complications. Many judges seem to favor those leaving a heterosexual marriage for a gay relationship, while disfavoring those leaving a gay relationship because of a religious conversion, even if he or she is a biological parent of the children involved. If the scenario becomes this dire, contact the Alliance Defending Freedom.

What if a Christian friend begins to embrace pro-gay theology?

Several books are influencing Christians to reconsider the historic Christian stance on same-sex marriage, including *Torn: Rescuing the Gospel from the Gays vs. Christians Debate* by Justin Lee; *God and the Gay Christian: The Biblical Case in Support of Same-sex Relationships* by Matthew Vines[6] and *A Letter to My Congregation* by Ken Wilson, a pastor in the Vineyard Church movement.[7] Each endorses only committed homosexual relationships. While we disagree with their conclusions, we recognize they are provocative, articulate and persuasive to many people.

Churches, pastors and parents need to know the arguments found in these works and how to respond. If someone is questioning, offer to read with them books on both sides of the issue. Many younger evangelicals wrongly assume that because they were raised *hearing* that homosexuality was wrong, they *know* the full truth about marriage and why it does not include same-sex relationships. In our experience, that simply is not true. Terrific resources that support natural marriage include *What Is Marriage? Man and Woman: A Defense* by Robert George, Ryan Anderson and Sherif Girgis; *Washed and Waiting: Reflections on Christian Faithfulness and Homosexuality* by Wesley Hill; and, of course, this book![8]

What if my church leadership shifts and decides to marry same-sex couples?

Christians should never leave a church because of a minor disagreement or conflict, but they may need to leave a church that is in grave error. Because endorsing same-sex marriage confuses the doctrine of the image of God and the first human institution initiated by God, it is a grave error. Of course, leaving should only come after all other options to lovingly confront and dissuade the church leadership have been exhausted.

What if my son or daughter thinks gays should be allowed to marry?

When I (Sean) was a teenager, I announced to my father, who has spent his life proclaiming and defending the Christian faith, than I wasn't sure I believed in Christianity anymore. He lovingly said that he respected my questions and offered to help me search any way he could. He encouraged me to hold on to my faith unless I was persuaded it was not true, and he assured me that he and my mom loved me regardless of the outcome.

That's a great way to handle any teenage questions about the faith. It's not a sin to question, and mentors should guide the questioning process. Be open, ask questions, give space, point to the best resources, and walk through the questions with the questioner. Above all, maintain the relationship.

*What if my boss asks me to celebrate the gay movement
or a same-sex marriage?*

Whether to have a piece of cake or say "congratulations" to a newly married gay or lesbian office colleague is a matter of a clear conscience before God. This would also apply, we think, to Christians who work for companies that have taken clear public stands in support of same-sex marriage. We don't think individuals need necessarily to feel personally responsible for the stance of their employers.

There are other cases where a supervisor, perhaps in the name of "team-building," requires employees to show support for same-sex marriage or a pro-LGBT cause by wearing a symbol or joining a gay pride event. Rights of conscience extend to the workplace, too, and no one should be forced to violate their conscience in order to keep their job. Know your rights, and if necessary, contact the Alliance Defending Freedom for advice.

What if I hear a fellow Christian "gay-bashing"?

In 1996, a white supremacist with an SS tattoo and a confederate flag shirt became separated from other Ku Klux Klan members at a rally in Ann Arbor, Michigan. A group protesting the rally chased him, and when he fell, began to beat him. Instinctively, 18-year-old Kiesha Thomas threw herself on the man to protect him. Kiesha is an African-American.[9]

Our faith requires us to defend anyone who is mistreated, even if we disagree with them. To do so, we may need to make the difficult decision to call out inappropriate words and actions from those on "our side." It's tempting to consider those more extreme than us as "quirky" or "intense," while assuming anyone who disagrees is "evil" and even "dangerous." So, we end up tolerating the extremist on our side, like a drunken uncle who shows up every Thanksgiving ("After all," we say, "he's family!"). But the moment the drunken uncle becomes abusive, tolerating him becomes enabling him. We must not, by our actions or our passivity, enable the mistreatment of the gay community.

What if I'm asked what I believe about same-sex marriage?

Whenever we talk about this issue, we risk being called "intolerant" or "hateful." Greg Koukl suggests that we can get ahead of the accusations by asking the following question before offering our opinion:

> You know, this is actually a very personal question you're asking, and I'd be glad to answer. But before I do, I want to know if you consider yourself a tolerant or an intolerant person. Is it safe to give my opinion, or are you going to judge me for my point of view? Do you respect diverse points of view, or do you condemn others for convictions that differ from yours?[10]

Asking this upfront makes it difficult for someone to dismiss our views as intolerant or judgmental without looking guilty of the same crimes. It's amazing how framing the discussion as one of mutual respect and *true* tolerance can change the dynamic of the entire interaction. We have both found that most people are willing to talk about this issue if they feel respected, understood and valued. So before you dive in and give your thoughts on this sensitive subject, make sure the person is truly tolerant and willing to respect people with different views than their own. And, of course, show the same respect in turn.

We should also be wise about *when* and *where* we choose to answer. Some issues, like the definition of marriage, are not suitable for short sound-bite discussions. Find sufficient time in a calm, non-threatening setting, and be prepared to listen as well as present. And don't preach in that setting. People have legitimate questions about this issue, and it takes time to work through them.

What if a conflict escalates?

Emotionally charged conversations tend to escalate. These words from Proverbs are wise: "A soft answer turns away wrath, but a harsh word stirs up anger" (15:1). If the person you are talking with gets angry, stay calm. Be intentional not to respond in the same tone of voice.

If a conflict does escalate, walk away. Consider saying something like this: "We clearly care deeply about this issue, but your friendship is very important. Let's take a break and maybe come back to this conversation another time."

Avoiding conflict is especially difficult when it happens online. A popular blogger once tweeted out a link to his article along with the sarcastic line, "Josh McDowell's son teaching people how to love." As a speaker and writer, I am used to criticism, but when I clicked on this link, I found a whole new level of personal vitriol from both Christians and non-Christians that surprised and saddened me.

Why the attacks? In 2008, as I sat on a panel at a large church, someone asked me how we should treat our gay friends. I emphasized that we are to love our gay friends just as we would love our non-gay friends, and then I told a story to indicate that part of friendship, as Paul says, is speaking the truth in love. The blogger included the story I told, but none of the context, making my response sound harsh and judgmental.

I was angry. Close friends told me to respond harshly and point out how the blogger had misrepresented me. Instead, I decided to wait for my emotions to cool and then wrote a personal letter to the blogger. I attempted to find common ground with the blogger and shared the full context of the video. I asked him to contact me first in the future before posting something so publicly critical.

To his credit, the blogger posted my entire letter and commented that though he still disagreed with me, he respected my approach and had misjudged my heart. Not everyone was satisfied, and I was still called homophobic, intolerant, exclusivistic, bigoted and even Talibanic! But many others said they appreciated my willingness to speak the truth in love.

We can also diffuse conflict by recognizing and respecting honesty and charity from those on the other side of this issue. For example, a group of same-sex marriage advocates released a statement in April 2014, after the forced resignation of Mozilla CEO Brendad Eich, entitled "Freedom to Marry, Freedom to Dissent: Why We Must Have Both." In it, they affirmed their "unwavering commitment to the values of the open society and to vigorous public debate."[11]

A few months earlier, same-sex marriage advocate Connor Friedersdorf stuck his neck out to defend Elaine Hugeunin from others calling her hateful and intolerant for refusing to photograph a same-sex wedding. Friedersdorf wrote, "I've never met the woman. None of us can look inside her heart. But her petition presents a perfectly plausible account of why she would refuse to photograph same-sex weddings for perfectly common religious reasons that have nothing to do with fear of gays, intolerance toward gays, or hatred of gay people."[12] This sort of statement advances the conversation, and we should acknowledge it.

Closing Thoughts . . .

These, obviously, are not the only scenarios we will face. As a Church and as a culture, we are headed into uncharted waters. But we need not despair. Yes, same-sex marriage *is* here. It will do us no good to run from culture, pretend this is not true or cry foul. The real question is, how will we respond? And "we" refers to *all* of us. Whether you are a pastor, parent, teacher, student or concerned member of the church, what will *you* do about it? Will you model biblical sexuality and marriage in your own life? Will you lovingly and graciously defend marriage? Will you help build a positive marriage culture? We will only positively influence lives and culture if *each* of us takes responsibility for the opportunities God has given us.

And let's remember that we need each other. The author of Hebrews wrote, "Let us hold fast the confession of our hope without wavering, for he who promised is faithful. And let us consider how to stir up one another to love and good works, not neglecting to meet together, as is the habit of some, but encouraging one another, and all the more as you see the Day drawing near" (Hebrews 10:23-25).

We are at a unique point in history when we can learn from the past and move forward, trusting God with confidence. There is a broken and hurting world that desperately needs the truth, the love and the hope of Jesus. Let's go!

Appendix A

What Followers of Jesus Who Struggle with Ongoing Same-Sex Attraction Need from the Church

One of our friends is a gifted academic and committed follower of Jesus. He also struggles with same-sex attraction. We asked him, "What do followers of Jesus who struggle with ongoing same-sex attraction need from the Church?"

First, we need the Church to recognize that "those people" are sometimes sitting in the second row. Homosexuality has become a litmus test for a bunch of things, from orthodoxy to a view of the Bible to one's worldview. As such, there's a tendency to think the Church is a besieged minority attacked by "homosexual activists." That's true to a point. But if you think about it, sexual brokenness happens to a lot of people, heterosexual and homosexual. Adultery, fornication and divorce are sins too, but they're talked about in church with much more pastoral sensitivity, as well as more room for hope and compassion.

Whether it's people who are "out and proud" and wish they weren't, people who are gay but chaste, or people who would be wary of any label, "they" are in the Church, desiring to be loved, to belong and to be faithful. Single people, hetero and homosexual, are often stigmatized by the marriage culture, left out or simply made to feel they're less than fulfilled. That's not the Bible; that's church people trying desperately to make people less messy than they are, or to fit them into stereotypical gender roles that don't come from Scripture either.

Second, we need the Church to realize that everyone is sexually broken. Long before gay marriage, heterosexually broken people were common and accepted in the Church. Adultery, fornication and divorce are much more common and, biblically speaking, much more problematic sins. Yet, the only time it seems church people want to "stand for marriage" is when it involves other people's sins, ones that make us uncomfortable. If we start where the Bible does in 1 John 1:9, and all acknowledge our sins, then we could all embrace Corinthians 6:11: "And such were some of you: but ye are washed, but ye are sanctified, but ye are justified in the name of the Lord Jesus, and by the Spirit of our God" (*KJV*). This should include divorcé(e)s, commitment-phobes, porn addicts, masturbators, adulterers, fornicators, gays and lesbians. In other words, all of us who are washed sinners.

Third, we need the Church to be willing to accept struggle. There's much to say about this point, but in essence it's simple: I want the Church to treat homosexual sex the same way it treats extramarital sex. Yes, it's a sin. And we, by God's grace, are to pick ourselves up, deal with the consequences, seek absolution and repentance, and move on. Classically speaking, sexual sin is in the same category as lust for food. By placing it in a special category, church people often reflect the same error as the gay liberation lobby—mistaking temptation and attraction for identity. No one does this, however, with gluttons at the local McDonald's. We are going to screw up. We have to create space for repentance and restoration.

Fourth, we need the Church to *not* move the goal posts. It isn't loving to lie. God has spoken clearly in Scripture, in tradition, in the natural order, and by human reason that sex is for heterosexual, covenant marriage only. If you change that, you not only are faithless to God but also to every person who lives chastely, whether gay or straight or in between.

Fifth, we need the Church to make room for baptismal family. We make the same error as the gay lobby if we equate love with sex. There are many different types of love and households with no sexual element: family affection, brotherhood, sisterhood, friendship, non-sexual partners in business or work, and companionate love. The Church too often asks attracted people to live a chaste life without helping them do it. Single must not mean alone, but in our culture it often does. If we ask gays and lesbians to forgo one kind of intimacy because it is (rightly) seen as disordered and incompatible with Scripture, then we must come around them to offer the tightest and most beautiful expression of family we have. That means valuing our gifts, affirming our successes, and recognizing our dignity as children of God and faithful members of the Church.

Finally, we need the Church to show us kindness. People attracted to the same-sex, yet seeking to remain chaste, are attempting something our culture says is impossible. And it is impossible without the support, love, pastoral guidance and accountability offered by a loving community who meets people where they bleed. The Master was always gentle with recovering sinners—which means all of us—and He asks us to stretch to grab the lost, the loneliest and the sinner in need of mercy so that He may lay the lost sheep on His shoulders and bring it home rejoicing. We too often announce the doctrine (correctly) without the pastoral sensitivity that meets people where they are. This is an urgent problem in a culture increasingly accepting of new gay family forms, increasingly broken and increasingly love hungry.

Appendix B

Answering Common Questions and Slogans About Same-Sex Marriage

Our friend Greg Koukl is the author of the book Tactics: A Game Plan for Discussing Your Christian Convictions.[1] *We asked him to apply his tactics to common questions about same-sex marriage.*

Isn't opposing same-sex marriage the same as opposing interracial marriage?

Simply put, no. Just because *objections* have been raised to both interracial marriage and same-sex marriage does not mean that the *circumstances* have been the same. They're not. In *Loving v. Virginia*, the U.S. Supreme Court struck down anti-miscegenation laws because "Marriage is . . . fundamental to our very existence and survival." This is not true of same-sex unions.

Objection to same-sex marriage is based on an observation of the natural order: "conjugal" husband/wife marriages begin the families that are the building blocks of civilization. Skin color is irrelevant to that biological, childbearing element of heterosexual unions. Sex, however—in the sense of both sexual activity and gender—is fundamental to that function. There is no difference between a black and a white human being, but there is an enormous difference between a man and a woman.

Curiously, those who *promote* same-sex marriage are the ones most like those who *opposed* interracial marriage in the past, since both positions subvert the clear, natural order in the same way. One says gender doesn't matter. The other said race does. Both are the exact opposite of the pattern of nature: gender matters in marriage and race does not. When it comes to marriage, nature is blind to skin color but not to gender.

Further, just because there's a *distinction* does not mean there's an unfair *discrimination*. No one would use this defense to answer opposition to polygamy or incestuous unions ("This is the same as opposing interracial marriage"). It's equally unhelpful here. It's also misleading. Same-sex marriage is not about including those wrongly excluded from an existing institution; it's about completely recasting that institution while continuing to use the same name.

> *How can you say that the love of two people of the same sex*
> *is any different than the love of a heterosexual couple?*
> *Don't you believe in marriage equality?*

Agreed, the love between people of the same sex may be just as profound as the love between people of opposite sexes. But love is not the issue here, is it?

In our culture, marriage is often *motivated* by love, yet marriage is not *defined* by love. If it were, then billions of people in the world who thought they were married were not. Most marriages have been arranged and many lack love, yet they are no less marriages. Love may percolate later, but only as a result of marriage, not the reason for it.

"For better or for worse" promises would not be needed either, nor any pledge at all since people in love naturally stay together. Rather, vows are made to sustain marriage when love wanes. A pledge keeps a family intact not for love, but for children.

The real issue with marriage licensing is not emotion, but function. The government does not care how a couple *feels* (it's not on the form), but rather how they *fit in* to the larger social context. Most pairings (as such), no matter how intimate, are inconsequential to social stability. However, long-term, monogamous, heterosexual unions as a group, as a rule and by nature, produce the next generation. They are, therefore, privileged, protected and regulated by culture because of their unique and vital role. Love may be the reason many *get* married, but it isn't the reason cultures *sanction* marriage. It may be a *constituent* of marriage, but it isn't the *purpose* of marriage.

No one in this discussion believes in unqualified "marriage equality" unless they promote polygamy, marriage of minors and a whole host of other exotic permutations. Instead, there should be equality of marriage for everyone *to whom the term "marriage" properly applies*. This would exclude children, close relatives, same-sex relationships, group unions, etc. Indeed, the concept of same-sex marriage never occurred until now because it was a contradiction in terms.

Why do you hate gay people?

Why assume that all those opposed to same-sex marriage are motivated by hate? I might ask, "Why do those supporting same-sex marriage hate people who don't?" but that would be unfair and uncharitable. Clearly, there is no reason to think that mere opposition to a view is driven by hatred, bigotry, intolerance or any other vice. Why, then, level the charge?

I suspect the reason is that this kind of name-calling is rhetorically expedient. People resort to it because they do not have anything more productive to say. Ridicule and name-calling are not arguments. It's unfortunate that so many think they are.

If marriage is about procreation, what about elderly or infertile couples getting married? We don't have laws against them.

It's easy to resist any suggestion that marriage and family are fundamentally connected to procreation. Clearly, not all families have children. Some marriages are barren, by choice or by circumstance. This proves nothing. The natural marriage/procreation connection is not nullified because in some cases children are not intended or even possible. The state protects conjugal marriage because of its *institutional* importance to culture. Pointing at exceptional cases doesn't nullify the general rule.

Also, any suggestion that there is a "ban" on "gay marriage" is misleading. There are no laws against it, so there is no "ban" on it. There simply is no legal provision for it. The state is not *hostile* to same-sex relationships. It simply does not *promote* them because it has no reason to.

When questions like these arise in conversation, is there a tactical approach you suggest so that the discussion is productive and fair?

I always favor using questions when maneuvering on issues like this. They're interactive and promote a friendly atmosphere. I use them to draw people out and to give them a chance to explain their own view more precisely so that I don't misunderstand them. Variations of the questions "What do you mean by that?" or "How did you come to that conclusion?" force the other person to think more carefully about his opinion, often for the first time.

Sometimes I use a question to make a point. For example, "Is marriage something that's *defined* or something that's *described*?" In other words, is marriage a cultural construct we can redefine at will (such as which side of the road we drive on), or a feature of reality we discover and describe (such as gravity)?

Proponents of same-sex marriage prefer the first option: marriage is flexible. My follow-up question is, "What is your principled argument, then, against polygamy, polyandry (multiple husbands), polyamory (group marriage) or any other creative combination?" If they say I'm being ridiculous, I'll agree. Those alternatives *are* ridiculous, but they follow from *their* view not *mine*. They're the ones who are saying marriage can be redefined any way we want. If marriage has a fixed, natural purpose, though, it's not infinitely flexible, certainly not malleable enough to include same-sex marriage.

Endnotes

Introduction

1. David Kinnaman and Gabe Lyons, *unChristian: What a New Generation Really Thinks about Christianity . . . and Why It Matters* (Grand Rapids, MI: Baker Books, 2007), pp. 92-93.
2. Richard John Neuhaus, "Telling the World Its Own Story," The Chuck Colson Center for Christian Worldview, July 2001. http://www.colsoncenter.org/search-library/search?view=searchdetail&id=21199 (accessed March 2014).

Part 1—What Marriage Is and Why It Matters

1. G. K. Chesterton, "The Superstition of Divorce," Free Republic, 1920. http://www.freerepublic.com/focus/f-religion/2883391/posts (accessed March 2014).

Chapter 1—What Just Happened to Our Culture?

1. David Von Drehle, "How Gay Marriage Won," *Time*, March 28, 2013, p. 22. A more detailed discussion of this time period is found in Evan Wolfson's book, *Why Marriage Matters: America, Equality, and Gay People's Right to Marry*, in the chapter titled, "Why Now?" (New York: Simon & Schuster, 2004), pp. 19-50.
2. Ibid. Statistics of approval for same-sex marriage are also taken from this article.
3. Ibid.
4. "The Outing" was the name of this fifty-seventh episode of *Seinfeld*, which first aired on February 11, 1993. See "The Outing," *Wikipedia*. http://en.wikipedia.org/wiki/The_Outing (accessed March 2014).
5. Susan Donaldson James, "When Gender Goes, Happiness Blooms in Marriage," *ABC News*, July 3, 2013. http://abcnews.go.com/Health/sex-marriage-gender-disappears-happiness-blooms/story?id=19560588 (accessed March 2014). See also Stephanie Pappas, "Gay Parents Better than Straight Parents? What Research Says," *Huffington Post*, October 27, 2011. http://www.huffingtonpost.com/2012/01/16/gay-parents-better-than-straights_n_1208659.html (accessed March 2014); Stephanie Pappas, "Legalizing Same-Sex Marriage May Improve Public Health," *LiveScience*, February 27, 2013. http://www.livescience.com/27501-legalized-same-sex-marriage-health.html (accessed March 2014); William Meezan and Jonathan Rauch, "Gay Marriage, Same-Sex Parenting, and America's Children," *The Future of Children*, vol. 15, no. 2, Fall 2005. http://futureofchildren.org/publications/journals/article/index.xml?journalid=37&articleid=108&sectionid=702 (accessed March 2014).
6. Evan Wolfson, "Samesex Marriage and Morality: The Human Rights Vision of the Constitution," April 1983. http://freemarry.3cdn.net/73aab4141a80237ddf_kxm62r3er.pdf (accessed March 2014).
7. Andrew Sullivan, "Here Comes The Groom: A (Conservative) Case For Gay Marriage," *New Republic*, August 28, 1989. http://www.newrepublic.com/article/79054/here-comes-the-groom (accessed March 2014).
8. Polygamy is one bride or groom marrying multiple spouses. Polyamory involves multiple partners of various genders being intimately involved with one another. For example, see Jillian Keenan, "Legalize Polygamy! No. I am not kidding," *Slate*, April 15, 2013, and Michael Carey, "Is Polyamory a Choice?" *Slate*, October 16, 2013.
9. As of December 4, 2013, Microsoft Word (version 14.3.8) still gave the red underline of shame to the word "polyamory."

10. Vermont was the first state to legally recognize civil unions for same-sex couples, but it did not refer to the unions as "marriage."

11. Justice Kennedy wrote the majority opinion of the United States Supreme Court in *United States v. Windsor*. He references the term "animus" in relation to the motivation for legislation against same-sex couples seeking the same rights as married heterosexual couples. This ruling is available at http://www.supremecourt.gov/opinions/12pdf/12-307_6j37.pdf (accessed March 2014). For an explanation of Justice Kennedy's rulings in relation to "animus," see Steven Goldberg, *Beyond Coercion: Justice Kennedy's Aversion to Animus*. http://scholarship.law.upenn.edu/cgi/viewcontent.cgi?article=1284&context=jcl (accessed March 2014).

12. Apparently, the famous quote—that Chesterton never actually said—was put in his mouth by John F. Kennedy. Chesterton did say something similar, to which Kennedy was most likely referring, in his book *The Thing* (Lanham, MD: Sheed and Ward, 1929). For a helpful explanation and the full quotation, see "Taking the Fence Down," The American Chesterton Society. http://www.chesterton.org/taking-a-fence-down/ (accessed March 2014).

Chapter 2—Beyond the Noise, Beyond the Heat: Starting at the Right Place

1. MOPS stands for Mothers of PreSchoolers.

2. For the best summary of these reasons, see Jennifer Roback Morse, "77 Non-religious Reasons to Support Man/Woman Marriage," *Ruth Institute*, 2010. http://www.ruthinstitute.org/77Reasons/ (accessed March 2014).

3. *Sphere Sovereignty* (p. 488), cited in James D. Bratt, ed., *Abraham Kuyper, A Centennial Reader* (Grand Rapids, MI: Eerdmans, 1998).

4. Owen Strachan, "Back to Your Posts: A Response to Dalrymple on Marriage," *Patheos*. http://www.patheos.com/blogs/thoughtlife/2012/11/back-to-your-posts-a-response-to-dalrymple-on-marriage/ (accessed March 2014).

5. See also Robert P. George, Timothy George and Charles W. Colson, *Manhattan Declaration: A Call of Christian Conscience*, November 20, 2009. http://manhattandeclaration.org/man_dec_resources/Manhattan_Declaration_full_text.pdf (p. 9).

6. The most prominent attempt to question the historic understanding of the Church in regards to the Bible's teaching on homosexuality has been by Matthew Vines. Vines first created a video of a sermon that went viral and more recently published the book *God and the Gay Christian: The Biblical Case in Support of Same-Sex Relationships* (Convergent Books, 2014). The sermon was entitled "The Gay Debate: The Bible and Homosexuality" (see .http://www.matthewvines.com/). Left-leaning journalist Leonard Pitts Jr. called the sermon "A masterwork of scriptural exegesis," though it is unclear what qualifies him to evaluate scriptural exegesis (quote taken from Vines's website). Among the many actual theologians who disagree are Wesley Hill, *Washed and Waiting: Reflections on Christian Faithfulness and Homosexuality* (Grand Rapids, MI: Zondervan, 2010); Richard B. Hays, "Homosexuality," *The Moral Vision of the New Testament* (New York: HarperCollins, 1996), chapter 16, pp. 379-406; and Alexander Pruss, *One Body: An Essay in Sexual Ethics* (University of Notre Dame Press, 2012).

7. See for example, Al Wolters, *Creation Regained: Biblical Basics for a Reformational Worldview*, second ed. (Grand Rapids, MI: Eerdmans, 2005); and Cornelius Plantinga Jr., *Engaging God's World: A Christian Vision of Faith, Learning, and Living* (Grand Rapids, MI: Eerdmans, 2002).

8. Liza Mundy, "The Gay Guide to Wedded Bliss," *Atlantic*, June 2013. http://www.theatlantic.com/magazine/archive/2013/06/the-gay-guide-to-wedded-bliss/309317/ (accessed March 2014).

9. Gunnar Andersson, et al., "The Demographics of Same-Sex Marriage in Norway and Sweden," Demography 43 (2006), pp. 79-98.

Chapter 3—What Is Marriage? Part One: What God Thinks

1. Both John (John 1:1-3) and Paul (Colossians 1:15-17) place Jesus in the beginning and describe Him as responsible for creation.

2. Cornelius Plantinga Jr., *Not the Way It's Supposed to Be: A Breviary of Sin* (Grand Rapids, MI: Eerdmans, 1995).

3. Rachel Held Evans, for example, makes this claim about femininity in her book, *A Year of Biblical Womanhood: How a Liberated Woman Found Herself Sitting on Her Roof, Covering Her Head, and Calling Her Husband "Master"* (Nashville, TN: Thomas Nelson, 2012). In a gimmicky sort of way, Evans rightly notes that Christians often take what is cultural and call it "biblical." In doing so, however, she makes the same mistake as her critics, only in the opposite direction: the confusion of roles with design. Roles are culturally determined; design is not. While many of those she critiques have wrongly elevated roles to the level of design, she reduces design to the level of roles.

4. Matthew Lee Anderson, "The Questions of Gay Marriage: How serious a concern is homosexuality?" *Mere Orthodoxy*. http://mereorthodoxy.com/how-serious-homosexuality/ (accessed March 2014).

5. Ibid.

6. Keep in mind that the first to hear this Genesis narrative were members of a just-freed nation of Hebrew slaves. Those who had just seen the defeat of the various gods they had been taught to worship in Egypt learn that there is just one God and that they are not His pawns but rather are in His image. Slaves are being told that they were made to be rulers. This is more than a theology lesson for them; it's a worldview lesson. They are learning that they live in a wholly different world than the world they had been acculturated to believe.

7. Note that the blessing in Genesis 1:28 includes instruction to fill and subdue the earth, not just the garden.

8. We are indebted to Frank Turek for this point. Frank shared the idea with John in a radio interview in 2013. It is available at www.breakpoint.org.

9. Not all non-marital sexual activity is treated as equally deviant. For example, while very little is said about the act of masturbation in the Bible, Jesus strongly condemns an adulterous mindset. In Romans 1, homoerotic behavior is among the signs of cultural decline and that God has given people over to the natural consequences of their own disordered passions. In Old Testament law, harsher penalties indicate what is considered more deviant behavior (e.g., adultery, incest, bestiality) and seems to correlate to how much a behavior deviates from God's design for marital sex. An interesting example is in Genesis 38, when Judah recognizes that his widowed daughter-in-law, though having prostituted herself, is more righteous than he, since he failed to require the next son to perform his duty to marry her (an act that would have both protected and provided for her as a widow).

10. It's interesting that immediately after Jesus affirms the creation account about marriage in Matthew 19, the text indicates that Jesus welcomes children that were brought to Him. Perhaps this is merely coincidental, but perhaps it is not. Perhaps some who were present were inspired to think about the value of children in light of the words Jesus used to conclude His sermonette on marriage: "Let the one who is able to receive this receive it" (v. 12).

11. We've heard him say this in numerous talks, but it is also quoted in Tim Barnett's article, "Is Same-Sex Marriage Really about Equality?" *Clear Thinking Christianity*. http://www.clearthinkingchristianity.com/blog/same-sex-marriage-really-about-equality (accessed March 2014).

12. Arthur C. Brooks, *Gross National Happiness: Why Happiness Matters for America—And How We Can Get More of It* (New York: Basic Books, 2008).

Chapter 4—What Is Marriage? Part Two: Leaving God Out of It

1. Justice Anthony Kennedy, *United States v. Windsor* (2013). http://www.supremecourt.gov/opinions/12pdf/12-307_6j37.pdf (accessed March 2014).

2. Friedrich Nietzsche, Walter Kaufmann & R. J. Hollingdale, trans., *The Will to Power* (New York: Vintage Books, 1968), p. 401.

3. Luc Ferry, *A Brief History of Thought: A Philosophical Guide to Living* (New York: Harper Perennial, 2011), p. 72.

4. It is true, of course, that the Bible includes stories of polygamy. We'd argue these are presented descriptively, not prescriptively. These marriages rarely, if ever, ended well (think of Jacob, David or Solomon) and are particularly hard on the women in the story (think Abraham and Hagar). The first report of polygamy is of Lamech in Genesis 4:23, who clearly is portrayed as an arrogant, murderous man. It's interesting that Noah, clearly portrayed as a righteous man within an evil culture, is monogamous (see Genesis 6:9 and 7:13).

5. Alexander R. Pruss, *One Body: An Essay in Christian Sexual Ethics* (Notre Dame, IN: Notre Dame, 2013). See also the chapters by Richard B. Hays, "Divorce and Remarriage" and "Homosexuality" in *The Moral Vision of the New Testament: Community, Cross, New Creation, a Contemporary Introduction to New Testament Ethics* (New York: HarperOne, 1996).

6. Flannery O'Connor, "Letter to Betty Hester," *This Day in Letters*, September 6, 1955. http://theamericanreader.com/6-september-1955-flannery-oconnor (accessed March 2014).

7. We aren't saying here that the Bible is true because other sources corroborate it; but if it is true, then we would expect other sources to corroborate it. Also, it doesn't mean that people will accept what is obviously true about marriage from the Bible or from other sources. Paul says in Romans 1 that people, at times, actively suppress the truth.

8. Maggie Gallagher, "(How) Will Gay Marriage Weaken Marriage as a Social Institution: A Reply to Andrew Koppelman," *University of St. Thomas Law Journal*: Vol. 2: Issue 1, Article 3, 2004, p. 46. http://ir.stthomas.edu/ustlj/vol2/iss1/3 (accessed March 2014). Most of the following section relies heavily on this article.

9. *Marriage and the Public Good: Ten Principles* (Princeton, NJ: The Witherspoon Institute, 2008), pp. 9-19. http://protectmarriage.com/wp-content/uploads/2012/11/WI_Marriage.pdf (accessed March 2014). The summary of the findings is taken from Sherif Girgis, Ryan T. Anderson and Robert P. George, *What Is Marriage? Man and Woman: A Defense* (New York: Encounter Books, 2012), p. 42.

10. Gallagher, "(How) Will Gay Marriage Weaken Marriage," p. 45. In a footnote to this statement, Gallagher describes a small number of exceptions.

11. It's true that in some states, after commitment has been demonstrated for an extended length of time, a couple is considered to be in a "common law" marriage. The fact that there is such a thing reinforces the need for societies to manage relationships that potentially produce children.

12. Gallagher, "(How) Will Gay Marriage Weaken Marriage," p. 37.

13. Even in "open marriages," which are a very bad idea in our opinion, a husband or wife still must answer to their spouse for sexual decisions. Most commonly, however, exclusivity means a commitment to only one other person.

14. A summary of the exchange was given by David Zurawik, "Ha-ha-ha! Who Gets the Last Laugh Now?" *The Baltimore Sun*, September 21, 1992. http://articles.baltimoresun.com/1992-09-21/features/1992265082_1_quayle-murphy-brown-ideology (accessed March 2014).

15. Isabel Sawhill, "20 years later, it turns out Dan Quayle was right about Murphy Brown and unmarried moms," *The Washington Post*, May 25, 2012. http://articles.washington post.com/2012-05-25/opinions/35457123_1_father-moves-marriage-biological-parents (accessed March 2014).

16. Barack Obama, "We Need Fathers to Step Up," *Parade*, June 16, 2011. http://www. parade.com/104895/presidentbarackobama/barack-obama-we-need-fathers-to-step-up/ (accessed March 2014).

17. John Wooden and Steve Jamison, *Wooden: A Lifetime of Observations and Reflections On and Off the Court* (Lincolnwood, IL: Contemporary Books, 1997), p. 18.

18. I (John) owe this clarification to Sharon Brooks Hodge, executive director of Black Family Preservation Group, Inc (www.blackfamilies.org). The enlightening comment was made in a private conversation on November 21, 2013.

19. Gallagher, "(How) Will Gay Marriage Weaken Marriage," p. 43.

Chapter 5—What Is Marriage? Part Three: The Tale of Two Definitions

1. Sherif Girgis, Ryan T. Anderson and Robert P. George, *What Is Marriage? Man and Woman: A Defense* (New York: Encounter Books, 2012).

2. Caitlin Flanagan, "Is There Hope for the American Marriage?" *Time*, July 2, 2009. http://content.time.com/time/magazine/article/0,9171,1908434,00.html (accessed March 2014).

3. Ibid.

4. Girgis, et al., *What Is Marriage?* p. 1. Other terms for this view include "natural marriage," "biological marriage" or "traditional marriage." Each nomenclature has its positives and negatives but all agree on the three basics: oneness, procreative potential and permanence.

5. A very thorough description of this point can be found in the chapter "One Flesh, One Body," in Alexander Pruss, *One Body: An Essay in Christian Sexual Ethics* (Notre Dame: University of Notre Dame Press, 2013), pp. 89-157.

6. Ibid.

7. Girgis, et al., *What Is Marriage?* p. 30.

8. A thorough discussion of the connection between marriage and procreation can be found in Patrick Lee, Robert P. George, and Gerard V. Bradley, "Marriage and Procreation: The Intrinsic Connection," *Public Discourse*, March 28, 2011. http://www.thepublic discourse.com/2011/03/2638/ (accessed March 2014).

9. Maggie Gallagher, "(How) Will Gay Marriage Weaken Marriage as a Social Institution: A Reply to Andrew Koppelman," *University of St. Thomas Law Journal*, pp. 43-44. http://ir.stthomas.edu/cgi/viewcontent.cgi?article=1047&context=ustlj (accessed March 2014).

10. Girgis, et al., *What Is Marriage?* p. 2. It is of course possible, and might even be common, that hate and animus accompany the exclusion of gays and lesbians from marriage. If so, then hate and animus are wrong. My point is just that one can reject the idea of same-sex marriage without being guilty of hate and animus. Brandon Ambrosino, a proponent of same-sex marriage, makes this point in his article, "Being Against Gay Marriage Doesn't Make You a Homophobe," *The Atlantic*, December 13, 2013. http://www.theatlantic.com/national/archive/2013/12/being-against-gay-marriage-doesnt-make-you-a-homophobe/282333/ (accessed 2014).

11. Gallagher, "(How) Will Gay Marriage Weaken Marriage," p. 53.

12. Ibid.

13. *Fox News*, "Iron Chef Cat Cora and Her Lesbian Partner Both Pregnant," March 10, 2009. http://www.foxnews.com/entertainment/2009/03/10/iron-chef-cat-cora-lesbian-partner-pregnant/ (accessed March 2014)

14. Girgis, et al., *What Is Marriage?* p. 1.

15. E. J. Graff, Andrew Sullivan, ed., "Retying the Knot," *Same-Sex Marriage: Pro and Con: A Reader* (New York: Vintage Books, 1997), article in chapter 4, pp. 135-138. Quoted in Gallagher, "(How) Will Gay Marriage Weaken Marriage?" pp. 60-61.

16. Graff and Sullivan, *Same-Sex Marriage: Pro and Con: A Reader*, pp. xxii-xxx. Quoted in Gallaghar, "(How) Will Gay Marriage Weaken Marriage?" p. 61.

17. Brandon Ambrosino, "Being Against Gay Marriage Doesn't Make You a Homophobe," *The Atlantic*, December 13, 2013. http://www.theatlantic.com/national/archive/2013/12/being-against-gay-marriage-doesnt-make-you-a-homophobe/282333/ (accessed March 2013).

18. Doug Mainwaring, "I'm Gay and I Oppose Same-Sex Marriage," *Public Discourse*, March 8, 2013. http://www.thepublicdiscourse.com/2013/03/9432/ (accessed March 2014).

19. Girgis, et al., *What Is Marriage?* p. 15. See pp. 15-19 for an elaboration of this argument.

20. This in no way relegates orphaned or abandoned children or children produced from non-marital sexual relationships to second-class status. To set apart the marriage relationship merely recognizes reality.

21. Loren Marks, "Same-sex parenting and children's outcomes: A closer examination of the American psychological association's brief on lesbian and gay parenting," *Social Science Research*, 2012, p. 14. http://dx.doi.org/10.1016/j.ssresearch.2012.03.006 (accessed March 2014). Cited in Ana Samuel, "The Kids Aren't All Right: New Family Structures and the 'No Differences' Claim," *Public Discourse*, June 14, 2012. http://www.thepublicdiscourse.com/2012/06/5640/#_edn7 (accessed March 2014).

22. Mark Regnerus, "How different are the adult children of parents who have same-sex relationships? Findings from the New Family Structures Study," *Social Science Research*, 2012, p. 6. http://dx.doi.org/10.1016/j.ssresearch.2012.03.009 (accessed March 2014).

23. For a thorough discussion of the limitations of various studies, see Ana Samuel, "The Kids Aren't All Right."

24. Greg Koukl, "What Should I Say If . . . Answering the Everyday Questions and Slogans about Same-Sex Marriage," see Appendix B of this book.

Chapter 6—The "Cosmological" Shift: How Same-Sex Marriage Got Here

1. Franz Lidz, "Jason Collins overwhelmed by enormous support for his announcement," *Sports Illustrated*, April 30, 2013. http://sportsillustrated.cnn.com/magazine/news/20130430/jason-collins-comes-out-gay-nba-day-1/ (accessed March 2014).

2. Jason Collins and Franz Lidz, "Why NBA center Jason Collins is coming out now," *Sports Illustrated*, April 29, 2013. http://sportsillustrated.cnn.com/magazine/news/20130429/jason-collins-gay-nba-player/#all (accessed March 2014).

3. Chris Strauss, "ESPN's Chris Broussard thinks Jason Collins is a sinner," *USA Today*, April 29, 2013. http://ftw.usatoday.com/2013/04/espns-chris-broussard-thinks-jason-collins-is-a-sinner/ (accessed March 2014).

4. Broussard's statement was posted via his Twitter account @Chris_Broussard, April 30, 2013. http://www.twitlonger.com/show/n_1rk1p7h (accessed March 2014).

5. Rod Dreher, "Sex After Christianity," *The American Conservative*, April 11, 2013. http://www.theamericanconservative.com/articles/sex-after-christianity/ (accessed March 2014). The phrase "cosmological shift" comes from Dreher also.

6. The Supreme Court of the State of New Mexico, *Elane Photography, LLC v. Vanessa Willock*, August 22, 2013, Docket Number 33,687. http://online.wsj.com/public/resources/documents/Photogopinion.pdf (accessed March 2014).

7. Rheana Murray, "Gay hair stylist drops New Mexico governor as client because she opposes same-sex marriage," *New York Daily News*, February 22, 2012. http://www.nydailynews.com/news/national/gay-hair-stylist-drops-new-mexico-governor-client-opposes-same-sex-marriage-article-1.1027072 (accessed March 2014).

8. Dreher, "Sex After Christianity."
9. Benjamin Wiker, *Moral Darwinism: How We Became Hedonists* (Downers Grove, IL: Inter-Varsity Press, 2002).
10. Margaret Sanger, *The Pivot of Civilization* (Lenox, MA: Hard Press, 2006), p. 104. Cited in Benjamin Wiker, *10 Books that Screwed Up the World: And 5 Others that Didn't Help* (Washington, DC: Regnery Publishing, Inc., 2008), p. 138.
11. Wiker, *Ten Books that Screwed Up the World*, p. 197. Wiker offers a much more complete picture of the deviance of Kinsey and his research team than space or standards of appropriateness will allow here.
12. For this point and the section that follows, I am indebted to S. Michael Craven, "Where the Battle Rages: The Sexualizing of America," *Battle for Truth*. http://www.battlefortruth.org/ArticlesDetail.asp?id=156 (accessed March 2014).
13. Quoted in Craven, "Where the Battle Rages: The Sexualizing of America."
14. Pamela Paul, *Pornified: How Pornography Is Damaging Our Lives, Our Relationships, and Our Families* (New York: Owl Books, 2005).
15. Craven, "Where the Battle Rages."
16. Mary Steichen Calderone, M.D., *The Family Book About Sexuality* (New York: Harper & Row, 1981). Cited in Craven, "Where the Battle Rages."
17. Brad Wilcox, "The Evolution of Divorce," *National Affairs* (Fall 2009).
18. Ibid.

Part 2— What We Can Do for Marriage

1. Deitrich Bonhoeffer, "Stations on the Road to Freedom," *Ethics,* sixth ed. (New York: Simon & Schuster, 2012), p. 19.

Chapter 7—This Is No Time for Escape and Christianity Is No Excuse

1. Some may argue that Buddhism calls people "into the moment," but that's not the same thing as cultural concern.
2. Dietrich Bonhoeffer, "Letter to Eberhard Bethge¾Reflections on Hitler," On Being with Krista Tippett, July 21, 1944. http://www.onbeing.org/program/ethics-and-will-god-legacy-dietrich-bonhoeffer/feature/letter-eberhard-bethge-reflections (accessed March 2014).
3. Eberhard Bethge, "My Friend Dietrich," *Christian History*, vol. 32, October 1, 1991. http://www.ctlibrary.com/ch/1991/issue32/3240.html (accessed March 2014).
4. The Epicureans believed that the gods were remote and detached and had lost interest in humanity. They could, therefore, live however they pleased. Unsurprisingly, Epicureanism often took the form of hedonism. The Stoics, on the other hand, were fatalists. They believed that the gods determined just about every detail of human life. Paul confronts both worldviews in this sermon.
5. For a fascinating history of prohibition in America, see Daniel Okrent, *Last Call: The Rise and Fall of Prohibition* (New York: Scribner, 2011).
6. Robert George, Timothy George and Chuck Colson, drafting committee, *Manhattan Declaration: A Call of Christian Conscience*, Manhattan Declaration Inc., November 20, 2009. http://manhattandeclaration.org/man_dec_resources/Manhattan_Declaration_full_text.pdf (accessed March 2014).

Chapter 8—Learning from the Past: A Movement Worth Examining

1. For a fascinating discussion on what movements are and how they form, see Eric Hoffer, *The True Believer: Thoughts on the Nature of Mass Movements* (New York: Time Inc., 1963).
2. "Inaugural Address by President Barack Obama," The White House, January 21, 2013. http://www.whitehouse.gov/the-press-office/2013/01/21/inaugural-address-president-barack-obama (accessed March 2014).

3. Marshall Kirk and Hunter Madsen, *After the Ball: How America Will Conquer Its Fear and Hatred of Gays in the '90s* (New York: Penguin, 1989), p. xv.

4. Ibid.

5. Ibid.

6. Ibid., p. 134.

7. Ibid., p. 379.

8. Ibid., pp. 19-23. We are not in any way suggesting that these are accurate or acceptable stereotypes. These were stereotypes described by Kirk and Madsen.

9. Ibid., p. 64.

10. Ibid., pp. 107-108. For a concise summary of the "wrong" and "right" beliefs and actions identified by Kirk and Madsen, see the chart in Kirk and Madsen's book.

11. Ibid., p. 149.

12. Ibid., pp. 152-153.

13. Ibid., p. 153.

14. Ibid., p. 178.

15. Ibid., p. 179.

16. Ibid., p. 187.

17. For a summary of the "conversation" and the full video, see Rob Bluey, "VIDEO: Heritage's Ryan Anderson Debates Marriage with Piers Morgan, Suze Orman" The Foundary. http://blog.heritage.org/2013/03/26/video-ryan-anderson-debates-marriage-with-piers-morgan-suze-orman/ (accessed March 2014).

18. Kirk and Madsen, *After the Ball*, p. 154.

19. Richard John Neuhaus, "Telling the World Its Own Story," *The Wilberforce Forum*. http://www.colsoncenter.org/search-library/search?view=searchdetail&id=21199 (accessed March 2014).

20. Ed Stetzer, "Preach the Gospel, and Since It's Necessary, Use Words," *Christian Post*, June 26, 2012. http://www.christianpost.com/news/preach-the-gospel-and-since-its-necessary-use-words-77231/ (accessed March 2014).

Chapter 9—First Things First: The Call to Repentance

1. Marshall Kirk and Hunter Madsen, *After the Ball: How America Will Conquer Its Fear and Hatred of Gays in the '90s* (New York: Penguin, 1989), p. 373.

2. Ross Douthat, "The Terms of Our Surrender," *The New York Times*, March 1, 2014 (emphasis his). http://www.nytimes.com/2014/03/02/opinion/sunday/the-terms-of-our-surrender.html?_r=0 (accessed March 2014).

3. Ibid.

4. According to the American Chesterton Society, "This story has been repeated so often about Chesterton that we suspect it is true. Also, it seems it is never told about any one other than Chesterton. What we have not found, however, is any documentary evidence for it." http://www.chesterton.org/discover-chesterton/frequently-asked-questions/wrong-with-world/ (accessed March 2014).

5. T. M. Moore, "Thoughts on the State of the Church." Personal email correspondence to John Stonestreet, February 15, 2014. Used by permission.

6. Chuck Colson, *The Faith: What Christians Believe, Why They Believe It, and Why It Matters* (Grand Rapids, MI: Zondervan, 2008), p. 225.

7. John Wesley, "Letter to William Wilberforce," February 24, 1791. Quoted in John D. Woodbridge and Frank A. James III, *Church History, Volume Two: From Pre-Reformation to the Present Day: The Rise and Growth of the Church in Its Cultural, Intellectual, and Political Context* (Grand Rapids, MI: Zondervan, 2013), p. 428.

8. Collin Hansen and John D. Woodbridge, *A God-Sized Vision: Revival Stories that Stretch and Stir* (Grand Rapids: Zondervan, 2010), pp. 179-187.

9. Romans 2:4.

10. Shane L. Windemeyer, "Dan and Me: My Coming Out as a Friend of Dan Cathy and Chick-fil-A," *Huffington Post,* January 28, 2013. http://www.huffingtonpost.com/shane-l-windmeyer/dan-cathy-chick-fil-a_b_2564379.html (accessed March 2014).

11. A crosier is the cross-shaped staff carried by a bishop to represent his leadership over the flock of Christ. The *New York Times* once referred to it in print as a "crow's ear." See John Stonestreet, "Crow's Ears and Fundamentalists: The Media Doesn't Get Religion," *Break-Point,* March 1, 2013. http://www.breakpoint.org/bpcommentaries/entry/13/21613 (accessed March 2014).

12. *The Book of Common Prayer: and Administration of the Sacraments and Other Rites and Ceremonies of the Church* (Oxford University Press, 1990), p. 352.

Chapter 10—The Church and Same-Sex Marriage: A To-Do List

1. For a thorough examination of the odd way in which the Supreme Court ruled on *Roe v. Wade* and the accompanying case (*Doe v. Bolton*) that resulted in the legalization of abortion on demand across the United States, see Clarke D. Forsythe, *Abuse of Discretion: The Inside Story of Roe v. Wade* (New York: Encounter, 2013).

2. See John Stonestreet, "A Brief History of the Pro-Life Movement: An Interview with Scott Klusendorf, Part 1," *BreakPoint.* http://www.breakpoint.org/features-columns/articles/entry/12/24765 (accessed March 2014).

3. "Fact Sheet: Induced Abortions in the United States," The Guttmacher Institute, February 2014. http://www.guttmacher.org/pubs/fb_induced_abortion.html (accessed March 2014).

4. *Time,* January 14, 2013.

5. Forsythe, *Abuse of Discretion,* pp. 62-68.

6. What we now know about life at its earliest stages has left us with obvious legal contradictions. We fight to save the lives of babies that, in many states and under different circumstances, could be legally ended. One who murders a pregnant woman is guilty of two counts of homicide, but one who killed the same child under the guise of "reproductive rights" is not even guilty of one homicide. The only difference is "choice."

7. Historically, graphic images have been an important aspect of activism against war, genocide and racism. The "shock and awe" approach of sideswiping unsuspecting women and children with abortion images negatively impacts public opinion, but the same images, when used prudentially in the right time and place, can change hearts and minds. For a discussion of this, see John Stonestreet, "A Time to Shock? Using Images of Abortion in the Public Square," *BreakPoint,* January 30, 2014. http://www.breakpoint.org/bpcommentaries/breakpoint-commentaries-archive/entry/13/24428 (accessed March 2014).

8. For example, Christopher Kaczor, *The Ethics of Abortion: Women's Rights, Human Life, and the Question of Justice* (London: Routledge, 2010); Francis J. Beckwith, *Defending Life: A Moral and Legal Case Against Abortion Choice* (Cambridge, UK: Cambridge University Press, 2007); Scott Klusendorf, *The Case for Life: Equipping Christians to Engage the Culture* (Wheaton, IL: Crossway, 2009); Pope John Paul II, *The Gospel of Life (Evangelium Vitae)* (Boston, MA: Pauline Books and Media, 1995).

9. Klusendorf calls this "The Age of Apologetics." See "A Brief History of the Pro-Life Movement."

10. I (John) heard Chuck Colson say this several times in his speeches, especially to his Centurions classes. The Centurions is a one-year training program founded by Colson to train believers in Christian worldview. See www.centurionsprogram.org.

11.

12. We highly recommend the primer by Nathan Hitchen, *You've Been {Framed}: a new primer for the marriage debate* (Philadelphia, PA: John Jay Institute, 2013). http://www.johnjay institute.org/docs/Marriage_Primer_Second_Edition.pdf (accessed March 2014). An early attempt to clarify a game plan for rebuilding a culture of marriage, this primer helpfully identifies the most critical areas of confusion and what might be done to overcome them.

13. Kate Briquelet, "Lesbian waitress in 'anti-gay' receipt flap fired," *New York Post*, December 7, 2013. http://nypost.com/2013/12/07/waitress-claiming-couple-didnt-tip-because-shes-gay-gets-fired/ (accessed March 2014).

14. Cavan Sieczkowski, "Mom's Homophobic Response to Gay Dads' Birthday Invite Was a Radio Show Hoax," *Huffington Post*, February 15, 2014. http://www.huffingtonpost.com/2014/02/15/gay-dad-birthday-invite-hoax_n_4794437.html?utm_hp_ref=gay-voices (accessed March 2014).

15. Alyssa Newcomb, "Lesbian Couple Charged with Staging Hate Crime," *ABC News*, May 19, 2012. http://abcnews.go.com/blogs/headlines/2012/05/lesbian-couple-charged-with-staging-hate-crime/ (accessed March 2014).

16. Stephen Jiminez, *The Book of Matt: Hidden Truths About the Murder of Matthew Shepard* (Hanover, NH: Steerforth Press, 2013).

17. Ross Douthat, "The Terms of Our Surrender," *New York Times*, March 1, 2014. http://www.nytimes.com/2014/03/02/opinion/sunday/the-terms-of-our-surrender.html?_r=0 (accessed March 2014). At the time of this writing, the revenge efforts have not yet reached the level of persecution, in our view.

18. Justin Lee, *Torn: Rescuing the Gospel from the Gays vs. Christians Debate* (Nashville, TN: Jericho Books, 2012), p. 3.

19. Rosaria Butterfield tells her story in her book *The Secret Thoughts of an Unlikely Convert: An English Professor's Journey into Christian Faith* (Pittsburgh, PA: Crown & Covenant Publications, 2012).

20. See Wesley Hill, *Washed and Waiting: Reflections on Christian Faithfulness and Homosexuality* (Grand Rapids, MI: Zondervan, 2010).

21. See, for example, Justin Lee, *Torn*.

22. See Wes Hill, *Washed and Waiting*.

23. See Proverbs 6:16-19 and Romans 1:21-32.

24. Nathan Hitchen suggests that marriage advocates need to leverage emotion, narrative, story, metaphor and meme. See "Marriage Counter-Messaging: An Action Plan" (Philadelphia, PA: The John Jay Institute, 2013). http://www.johnjayinstitute.org/docs/Action_Plan2.pdf (accessed March 2014).

25. See the full video at http://piersmorgan.blogs.cnn.com/2013/12/06/rick-warren-on-homosexuality-i-fear-the-disapproval-of-god-more-than-i-fear-your-disapproval-or-the-disapproval-of-society/.

26. Taken from Michael Bauman, "A Non-Religious Case Against Same-Sex Marriage," The Imaginative Conservative. http://www.theimaginativeconservative.org/2013/04/a-non-religious-case-against-same-sex-marriage.html (accessed March 2014).

Chapter 11—Giving Marriage Back to the World: Suggestions for the Long Haul

1. Matt Walsh, "I've been divorced four times, but homosexuals are the ones destroying marriage," *The Matt Walsh Blog*, February 4, 2014. http://themattwalshblog.com/2014/02/04/ive-been-divorced-four-times-but-homosexuals-are-the-ones-destroying-marriage/ (accessed March 2014). Walsh clarifies that the title is tongue-in-cheek. He has only been married one time.

2. Margaret Mead, *Coming of Age in Samoa: A Psychological Study of Primitive Youth for Western Civilization* (New York: William Morrow and Company, 1928). Mead wasn't solely responsible for this myth.

3. See, for example, Derek Freeman, *Margaret Mead and Samoa: The Making and Unmaking of an Anthropological Myth* (New York: Penguin, 1986). Or for a more accessible critique of Mead, see Benjamin Wiker's chapter, "Coming of Age in Samoa," from *10 Books that Screwed Up the World: And 5 Others that Didn't Help* (Washington, DC: Regnery Publishing, 2008), pp. 177-194.

4. See, for example, Sarah Ruden, *Paul Among the People: The Apostle Reinterpreted and Reimagined in His Own Time* (New York: Image Books, 2010), pp. xix, 147ff.

5. Mark Regnerus, "Sex Is Cheap: Why young men have the upper hand in bed, even when they're failing in life," *Slate,* February 25, 2011. http://www.slate.com/articles/double_x/doublex/2011/02/sex_is_cheap.single.html. Also, see "The Economics of Sex: It's a Tough Market Out There" from the Austin Institute for the Study of Family and Culture. http://www.austin-institute.org/wp-content/uploads/2014/02/V10-Resource-Guide.pdf (accessed March 2014). Though Regnerus didn't invent the phrase "the economics of sex," he has offered the most accessible explanation.

6. A 2011 report of the National Institute of Population and Social Security Research found that over 25 percent of Japanese males aged 16 to 24 had no interest in sex or "found it appalling." For more on this bizarre phenomenon, see Max Fisher, "Japan's sexual apathy is endangering the global economy," *The Washington Post*, October 22, 2013. http://www.washingtonpost.com/blogs/worldviews/wp/2013/10/22/japans-sexual-apathy-is-endangering-the-global-economy/ (accessed March 2014).

7. See, for example, the summary of research provided in Lois M. Collins, "Why Dads Matter: A third of American children are growing up in homes without their biological fathers," *The Atlantic,* February 23, 2014. http://www.theatlantic.com/health/archive/2014/02/why-dads-matter/283956/ (accessed March 2014).

8. See Krishnadev Calamur, "Iceland's Plan to Ban Online Porn Sparks Outrage," *National Public Radio,* February 28, 2013. http://www.npr.org/blogs/thetwo-way/2013/02/28/173187642/icelands-plan-to-ban-online-porn-spurs-outrage (accessed March 2014).

9. See Bruno Waterfield, "MEPs to vote on EU 'ban on all forms of pornography,'" *The Telegraph,* March 8, 2013. http://www.telegraph.co.uk/technology/news/9917189/MEPs-to-vote-on-EU-ban-on-all-forms-of-pornography.html (accessed March 2014).

10. See "Online Pornography to Be Blocked by Default, PM Announces," *BBC,* July 22, 2013. http://www.bbc.com/news/uk-23401076 (accessed March 2014).

11. See "The Decline of Marriage and Rise of New Families," *The Pew Research Center*, November 18, 2010. http://pewsocialtrends.org/files/2010/11/pew-social-trends-2010-families.pdf (accessed March 2014).

12. A terrific exception is the film *Irreplaceable* and the accompanying small-group study *The Family Project: A Divine Reflection* (Colorado Springs, CO: Focus on the Family, 2014). www.familyproject.com (accessed March 2014).

13. "Confessions of an Ex-Evangelical, Pro-SSM Millennial," quoted by Rod Dreher, *The American Conservative*, February 27, 2014. http://www.theamericanconservative.com/dreher/ex-evangelical-pro-gay-millennial/ (accessed March 2014).

14. Malachi 2:16, according to the *Revised Standard Version*, "For I hate divorce, says the Lord the God of Israel, and covering one's garment with violence, says the Lord of hosts." According to the *English Standard Version*, it reads: "For the man who does not love his wife but divorces her, says the Lord, the God of Israel, covers his garment with violence, says the Lord of hosts."

15. For a summary of the report, see Jennifer Glass, "Red states, blue states, and divorce: Understanding the impact of conservative protestantism on regional variation in

divorce rates," *Council on Contemporary Families,* January 16, 2014. http://www.contemporary families.org/impact-of-conservative-protestantism-on-regional-divorce-rates/ (accessed March 2014).

16. See Charles E. Stokes, "Findings on Red and Blue Divorce Are Not Exactly Black and White," *Family Studies: The Blog of the Institute for Family Studies,* January 22, 2014. http://family-studies. org/findings-on-red-and-blue-divorce-are-not-exactly-black-and-white/ (accessed March 2014).

17. For a thorough examination of the cultural impact of the birth control pill, see Mary Eberstadt, *Adam and Eve After the Pill: Paradoxes of the Sexual Revolution* (San Francisco, CA: Ignatius Press, 2013).

18. The key word here is "planning." We are not condemning any families who wish to have children but cannot due to infertility or other medical conditions. Infertility is a tragic consequence of the fall, and couples that experience it deserve kindness and compassion. They should never be made to feel like second-class citizens or have their marriages portrayed as somehow less valuable than others.

19. For a startling example of violating the law of non-contradiction in this regard, see Jenell Paris, "Both Chastity and Contraception: A Sacred Compromise," *Christianity Today,* April 27, 2012. http://www.christianitytoday.com/ct/2012/aprilweb-only/chastity-contraception.html (accessed March 2014). Matthew Lee Anderson offered a helpful response in his piece, "A Hill to Die On: Evangelicals, Contraception, and the Integrity of our Witness," *Mere Orthodoxy,* April 30, 2012. http://mereorthodoxy.com/evangelicals-contraception-integrity/ (accessed March 2014).

20. Preventing conception but never through abortion however.

21. For a description of this idea in Augustine's thoughts and its influence on Christian theology, see Matt Jenson, *The Gravity of Sin: Augustine, Luther and Barth on* 'homo incurvatus in se' (London: T & T Clark, 2006).

22. Oscar Wilde, *The Picture of Dorian Gray* (Originally printed in 1890. Reprinted by Spear Press, 2013).

23. "Hearing on the Brain Science Behind Pornography Addiction and the Effects of Addiction on Families and Communities," Senate Committee on Commerce, Science and Transportation, November 18, 2004. http://www.ccv.org/wp-content/uploads/2010/04/Judith_Reisman_ Senate_Testimony-2004.11.18.pdf (accessed March 2014).

24. An updated report on pornography use can be obtained from Covenant Eyes, an online accountability ministry committed to helping Christians defeat porn addiction. See "250+ Facts and Stats About Pornography," Covenant Eyes. http://www.covenanteyes.com/pornog raphy-facts-and-statistics/ (accessed March 2013).

25. Mary Anne Layden, *The Social Costs of Pornography: A Statement of Findings and Recommendations* (Princeton, NJ: Witherspoon Institute, 2010).

26. See Josh McDowell's extensive research and resources on pornography at http://www.just 1clickaway.org.

27. Mark Regnerus, "Porn Use and Supporting Same-Sex Marriage," *Public Discourse,* December 20, 2012. http://www.thepublicdiscourse.com/2012/12/7048 (accessed March 2014).

28. For information on "Weekend to Remember" events, go to http://www.familylife.com/weekend.

29. For information on "The Family Project" study series, go to http://www.familyproject.com/.

30. For information on Summit Ministries, visit www.summit.org.

Chapter 12—So, What Now? Guidance for Everyday Questions

1. This story was told to us by a Christian school administrator who wishes to remain anonymous.

2. See Eric Metaxas, "When Life Ain't Fair: Christians, the Culture, and Grace," *BreakPoint,* March 10, 2014. http://www.breakpoint.org/bpcommentaries/entry/13/24724 (accessed March 2014).

3. See John Stonestreet, "Baking Cakes for Caesar: Why We Need Freedom to Say 'No,'" *Breakpoint,* March 3, 2014. http://www.breakpoint.org/bpcommentaries/entry/13/24666 (accessed March 2014).

4. See http://alliancedefendingfreedom.org/ (accessed March 2014).
5. See http://www.becketfund.org/ (accessed March 2014).
6. Matthew Vines, *God and the Gay Christian: The Biblical Case in Support of Same-Sex Relationships* (New York: Convergent Books, 2014). Vines is also the founder of The Reformation Project, a Bible-based, Christian non-profit organization that seeks to reform church teaching on sexual orientation and gender identity. See www.reformationproject.org (accessed March 2014).
7. Ken Wilson, *A Letter to My Congregation: An Evangelical Pastor's Path to Embracing People Who Are Gay, Lesbian, and Transgender into the Company of Jesus* (Canton, MI: David Crum, 2014).
8. We also recommend Aligned Grace Resources, a ministry designed to help churches promote gender wholeness. See www.alignedgraceresources.org.
9. For the full story and video of Thomas's heroic act, see Rhonesha Byng, "The Story of this Black Teen Who Protected a White Man From an Angry Mob Continues to Inspire," *Huffington Post,* October 29, 2013. http://www.huffingtonpost.com/2013/10/29/keshia-thomas-black-teen-white-man-kkk-rally_n_4175020.html (accessed March 2014).
10. Gregory Koukl, "Homosexuality: Giving Your Point of View." http://www.str.org/articles/homosexuality-giving-your-point-of-view#.U2FqnqIz3Kc (accessed March 2014).
11. "Freedom to Marry, Freedom to Dissent: Why We Must Have Both," *Real Clear Politics* (April 22, 2014). http://www.realclearpolitics.com/articles/2014/04/22/freedom_to_marry_freedom_to_dissent_why_we_must_have_both_122376.html (accessed April 2014).
12. See, for example, Connor Friedersdorf, "Refusing to Photograph a Gay Wedding Isn't Hateful," *The Atlantic,* March 5, 2014. http://www.theatlantic.com/politics/archive/2014/03/refusing-to-photograph-a-gay-wedding-isnt-hateful/284224/ (accessed March 2014).

Appendix B— Answering Common Questions and Slogans About Same-Sex Marriage
13. Greg Koukl, *Tactics: A Game Plan for Discussing Your Christian Convictions* (Grand Rapids, MI: Zondervan, 2009).

About the Authors

Sean McDowell is a gifted communicator with a passion for reaching the younger generation with the gospel message. He earned his Ph.D. in Apologetics and Worldview Studies from Southern Baptist Theological Seminary and is a professor at Biola University in the apologetics program. Sean is the author or coauthor of fifteen books, including *The Apologetics Study Bible for Students*. He travels widely, speaking at camps, churches, universities and conferences.

John Stonestreet is Executive Director of the Chuck Colson Center for Christian Worldview, as well as the cohost with Eric Metaxas of *Breakpoint*, the Christian worldview radio program founded by the late Chuck Colson. John is a sought-after speaker at conferences, colleges and churches on areas of faith and culture, theology and apologetics. He holds degrees from Trinity Evangelical Divinity School and Bryan College and is the coauthor of *Making Sense of Your World: A Biblical Worldview*.

www.breakpoint.org
Twitter: @jbstonestreet

Surrender the Secret and Be Set Free

An estimated one in three women of childbearing age has had an abortion. You probably know at least one of them. She may be your sister, your daughter, your friend or even your mother. She may be you.

After an abortion, many women carry a heavy burden of silence and heartache. Some struggle for years with repressed memories, guilt, shame and depression. Others feel they are not allowed to talk about their experience, especially in church. But healing can happen when the painful secret of abortion is surrendered to God for His glory. In *A Surrendered Life*, you will:

- Understand why women and men make a choice for abortion

- Learn how post-abortion heartbreak can show up in your life or the lives of your loved ones

- Discover the eight steps to healing from an abortion

- Get practical tools to guide a discussion about abortion

- Find out how to make a difference for women and children in your home, church and community

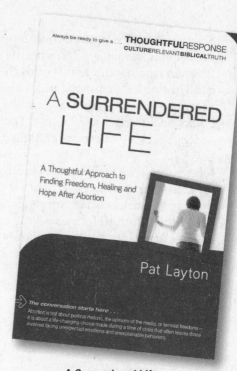

A Surrendered Life
Thoughtful Response Series
Patricia K. Layton
978.08010.18336

Thousands of women around the world have found healing from the emotional, spiritual and even physical scars abortion leaves behind. This unforgettable book will guide you or someone you love to surrender the secret and find hope for the future.

Available wherever books are sold